Inquiry Learning Through Librarian-Teacher Partnerships

Violet H. Harada
Joan M. Yoshina

Linworth
PUBLISHING, INC

Your Trusted
Library-to-Classroom Connection.
Books, Magazines, and Online

Library of Congress Cataloging-in-Publication Data

Harada, Violet H.
  Inquiry learning through librarian-teacher partnerships / Violet H. Harada and Joan M. Yoshina.
    p. cm.
  Includes bibliographical references and index.
  ISBN 1-58683-134-8 (pbk.)
  1. Questioning. 2. Teaching teams--United States. 3. School libraries--United States. 4. Curriculum planning--United States. I. Yoshina, Joan M. II. Title.
  LB1027.44.H37 2004
  371.14'8--dc22

                                    2004000662

Author: Violet H. Harada and Joan M. Yoshina

Published by Linworth Publishing, Inc.
480 East Wilson Bridge Road, Suite L
Worthington, Ohio 43085

ISBN: 1-58683-134-8

5 4

Table of Contents

Table of Figures and Templates

Templates

Acknowledgments

This book is a sum total of our thirty years of experience working with hundreds of educators in Hawaii and across the nation. Their willingness to share their successes and failures with us served as the seeds for this text. In particular, we thank the faculty of Mililani Mauka Elementary School for their contributions to the numerous classroom examples in this text, and to Betty Mow, who as principal inspired an inquiry-focused vision at that school.

Special thanks also go to graduate students in the University of Hawaii's Library and Information Science Program, who read and commented on excerpts of our work in progress, and to student aides in the program, who provided invaluable technical assistance.

Importantly, we thank professional colleagues in the field, who have supported and challenged our work including Carol Kuhlthau, Barbara Stripling, Jean Donham, Marjorie Pappas, Anne Tepe, Gail Bush, Sharon Coatney, Ken Haycock, Dave Loertscher, Jacqueline Mancall, Danny Callison, Debbie Abilock, Claire Sato, and Jean Sumiye.

Finally, we extend our warm appreciation to Judi Repman, who guided us through the pangs of birthing a first book. We express our deepest gratitude to Byron and Wayne, our spouses, who provided unfailing support when manuscript deadlines meant weeks of takeout dinners and additional household chores for them.

About the Authors

Violet H. Harada

Violet H. Harada is an associate professor in the Library and Information Science Program at the University of Hawaii where she also coordinates the specialization for school library media preparation. In her thirty-year career, she has been a secondary English teacher, an elementary school library media specialist, a state level administrator, and a curriculum designer. In her current research and publications, she focuses on inquiry-based approaches to information seeking and use and on the dynamics of collaborative learning. She and Joan Yoshina received an AASL/Highsmith research grant for their work in journal writing with young students engaged in information seeking. Violet also coordinated a Hawaii Partnerships for Learning project, which was funded by an AASL/ABC-CLIO leadership grant.

Joan M. Yoshina

Joan M. Yoshina recently retired from the Hawaii Department of Education after thirty-four years as an elementary and high school teacher, a language arts specialist, and a library media specialist. She worked in both elementary and middle school libraries on Oahu. Her last assignment was in a new, state-of-the-art elementary school library media center, which she helped to design. As a practicum librarian, she has mentored a number of Hawaii library media specialists. Joan has also published articles on the information search process and integrated instruction, guest lectured at the University of Hawaii, and presented her work at both local and national conferences.

Introduction

Picture This

▶ *In a first grade classroom in Orchard Park, New York, excitement runs high as the students wrestle with the question, "What pet should our class adopt for the classroom?" The youngsters gather information from library books and encyclopedias and from interviewing other students on campus. They graph their findings and post charts around the classroom. A local veterinarian offers tips on the proper feeding and care of different pets. The students even write letters to the local zoo for advice. Their final choice for a classroom pet: a guinea pig that the youngsters name Whiskers (Marriott, 2002).*

Fourth grade students in Jessamine County, Kentucky, read about the strip mining companies and their plan to cut the tip of Black Mountain, the highest peak in Kentucky. They are concerned about the environmental issues involved. They ask themselves, "What happens if the mountain is cut? Is this a good or bad thing?" Driven by a desire to learn more, they comb the newspapers for accounts about the proposed action, make a site visit, and interview the coal mining families that make a living in this region. Students synthesize their findings and present impassioned, well-documented testimonies to the state legislature in an effort to save Black Mountain. The end result: Their pleas are heard; the legislature passes a bill to stop the proposed action. The class also receives a Kentucky Earth Day Award and the President's Environmental Youth Award (Adams & Greenlief, 2001).

When middle school students in Hillsborough, California, discover through the news that 170 countries are convening in Japan to discuss global warming, they engage in their own investigation of this controversial issue. The big question that emerges is, "Why should we be concerned about global warming?" In a simulated project, students assume the roles of delegates and lobbyists representing corporate as well as health and environmental groups. They study the complicated economic, political, and scientific implications of the topic. Emotions often run high as the students really get into their roles and discover that there are conflicting viewpoints about the nature and impact of global warming. Ultimately, they stage a Conference on Climate Change that mirrors the Kyoto event. Parents and community visitors are invited to the students' conference. The culminating experience: After weeks of information searching via the Web and other sources, the students, dressed in character, present their findings in the form of persuasive speeches and negotiated solutions. They also send e-mail to their Congressional representatives and to the President and Vice-President of the United States (Abilock & Lusignan, 1998).

Middle and high school students and teachers in Maui County, Hawaii, have decided to adopt a waterfowl sanctuary near their schools as a "laboratory" for learning and for practicing responsible stewardship. Originally established by Hawaiian royalty as a fishing pond, the area suffered extensive loss in size and in water flow during World War II and under subsequent military control. Recently classified as a National Wildlife Refuge, the pond will undergo a major restoration effort. After visiting the sanctuary, teachers and students asked, "What happened to this pond? Why and how did this happen? What can we do about this?" The vision: School teams plan to partner with scientists from the Department of Land and Natural Resources in a ten-year project to restore the endangered flora and fauna. In the process, students will engage in hands-on experiences with scientists as mentors. They will collaborate on investigations, develop criteria for collecting data, devise procedures to control variables, conduct studies, and report their findings (L. Ogata, personal communication, May 20, 2003).

Elements of Inquiry Learning

What makes each of the above snapshots so compelling? Several factors are clearly evident:

- Learning is inspired and purposeful.
- Real world problems shape the curriculum.
- Big questions drive the projects.
- Learning extends beyond the classroom and school.

The bottom line: All of these projects nurture inquiry and deep thinking. They provoke and challenge students to go beyond textbooks and easy answers.

There is another less visible but crucial ingredient in each of the four snapshots — each project requires the collaborative energy of educators working in teams. In each instance, classroom teachers are working with other staff, notably the library media specialist, in developing inquiry learning opportunities. The library media specialist plays a key role in helping students focus their investigations, develop relevant questions, retrieve and evaluate data, and create meaningful presentations of newly gained knowledge.

Benefits of Engaging in Inquiry Learning

Teams that engage in inquiry learning invariably cite the following as major benefits for their students:

- Increased self-direction.
- Higher levels of comprehension.
- Growth in interpersonal skills and teamwork.
- Greater motivation about what they are learning.

One teacher and librarian team noted the following in their team journal:

> We now realize that when questions come from the children, they are much more powerful and purposeful than teacher-generated ones. The children are also encouraged to raise new questions that surface as a result of the information they are gathering. When students are part of the collaborative team, they help to set goals and they problem-solve how to meet these goals. If students are involved in the planning and learning process, it becomes much more meaningful for them. It is no longer the teacher's plan but it is OUR plan.

Students themselves have commented on the difference in how they are learning. A sixth grade student said:

> I really like this new way of learning. I help decide what to focus on in my project (I bet I am the only one in sixth grade that is choosing this focus). This means I can teach everyone else something new! It's not like we use only the textbook and do homework answers (BORING!!). We use all kinds of resources. I even talk to people outside the school about my project. Best of all, I don't have to do stupid reports. Beth and I are planning a skit for our project and we are going to put it on for second graders. Is that cool, or what!

"No Child Left Behind" and Inquiry Learning

Today's public schools face the challenge of the overwhelming mandates of *No Child Left Behind* (U.S. Department of Education, 2002). They are grappling with state testing and national assessment, the tracking of yearly progress, and rewards and sanctions that are wrapped into accountability measures at the state, district, as well as school levels.

NCLB outlines complex testing and accountability provisions; however, it does not prescribe specific teaching interventions that would make successful learning happen. A very real question that schools might ask would be does inquiry learning help us achieve our NCLB targets? Our answer is yes. We feel this approach to teaching and learning helps schools meet the following crucial requirements of NCLB:

The tests must measure student proficiencies in meeting state academic standards. Inquiry learning should clearly address standards in the various disciplines as well as in information literacy. In this text we present numerous examples of projects aligned with various state and national standards.

Standards (and tests) must measure key disciplinary concepts and higher order thinking skills. Inquiry learning emphasizes thematic and issues approaches to learning. This type of learning moves away from activities and tasks at the recall level to projects requiring the application of concepts and the synthesis, interpretation, and evaluation of information. We provide in-depth samples of projects that reflect these approaches to learning in this book.

While state tests and national assessment are key pieces in the accountability scheme, NCLB also encourages a comprehensive data system that includes local and teacher-developed assessments. A critical component in inquiry learning is the identification of learning goals and the development of assessment criteria to measure the desired learning outcomes. This type of ongoing and rigorous assessment can contribute to a rich profile or portfolio of the individual learner as well as groups of learners. In this book, we describe possible assessment strategies and provide classroom and library examples.

Finally, NCLB stresses research-based approaches to learning that lead to higher student achievement. Inquiry learning, which is based on constructivist principles, has a substantial body of research supporting it. Throughout this text, we make connections with key research and publications that highlight best practices and related studies.

The fundamental questions that schools must ask themselves are: What do the tests really tell us about student achievement? What implications do the test results have for our present curriculum? What implications do they have for our teaching? What changes are critical?

How This Book Is Organized

We address two overarching questions in this book:

- What is worth learning?
- How do we make this learning happen?

In dealing with these questions, we emphasize the following important points:

- Inquiry as a critical approach to learning.
- Student outcomes as the target in teaching.
- Library media specialists as key partners in curriculum planning.

The individual chapters deal with the following aspects of inquiry learning and the collaborative work involving the library media specialist. Each chapter is organized around key questions with explanations and examples throughout.

Chapter 1 provides an overview of the school environment in which inquiry learning is the focus. It describes how such a school differs from a conventional one and the role of the library media specialist in this school.

Chapter 2 defines the essential elements of an inquiry curriculum. It emphasizes the importance of questions that drive substantive learning.

Chapter 3 deals with school teams working collaboratively. It examines what makes these partnerships survive and thrive.

Chapter 4 zeroes in on two possible approaches to inquiry-focused instruction: 1) starting with themes or large concepts and 2) starting with problems or issues. It provides detailed explanations and scenarios of how both approaches are used in inquiry-focused projects.

Chapter 5 centers on assessing student learning in inquiry-focused projects. It describes different assessment tools and gives examples of the tools in practice.

Chapter 6 presents instructional strategies that can be used in these projects. It addresses the importance of dealing with diverse student needs and how technology provides a valuable tool for teaching and learning.

Chapters 7 through 9 highlight examples of inquiry-focused units, one each at the elementary, middle, and high school levels. Each example is organized in a template format for easier reading.

Chapter 10 returns full circle to the notion of building a school-wide approach to inquiry learning. It identifies specific action strategies to consider and a detailed scenario of how the strategies might be used in a school.

An extensive bibliography identifies the references used in this book. The list also provides a useful starting point for more information on various aspects of inquiry learning.

Who Might Use This Book

Inquiry learning requires planning and teaching as teams. While we highlight the collaborative effort of classroom teachers and the library media specialist, we also acknowledge the contributions of other critical team members including the technology coordinator and the administrator. For teams designing inquiry learning, the book provides guidelines for creating learning that results in important student achievement. It identifies research-based strategies and tools to strengthen collaborative instructional planning and presents practical suggestions for integrating information literacy with the school's academic program.

1 Identifying the Inquiry-Based School

What Does an Inquiry-Based School Look Like?

There is growing concern among educators that, for all our efforts at reform, students are not able to demonstrate the depth of understanding that they need to confront real-world problems. While content knowledge and skills are important and necessary targets for teaching and learning, we also need to focus on the thinking skills and habits of mind that lead to greater understanding. This is the defining quality of an inquiry-based learning environment.

To get a true feeling for what such an environment looks like, we must observe what occurs in a classroom. Here is a possible scenario.

> ## This chapter:
> - Identifies characteristics of an inquiry-based school.
> - Compares and contrasts the practices of inquiry-based and conventional learning environments.
> - Suggests action strategies in creating an inquiry-based school.
> - Discusses the role of the library media program in such an environment.

▶ *Fifth graders are studying colonization as part of a year-long thematic investigation of "change over time" that correlates with state content standards in social studies. In this unit, their framing question is, "How did colonization bring about change?" This question is posted on a large sheet of newsprint in the classroom. Students work in teams at tables, at the computers, and at the whiteboard on various stages of their projects. One team is composing a "fifth grade compact" akin to the Mayflower Compact. Another team is preparing a pictorial timeline of the period, which will be displayed in the library media center. A third group is working on their living museum presentation of life in colonial America, which will be staged at the school's Learning Fair. Throughout the unit, students move back and forth between classroom, computer lab, and library media center as they wrestle with:*

- *refining their research questions.*
- *using primary sources such as ships' logs and journals of colonial leaders.*
- *retrieving information that satisfies their needs.*
- *generating more questions.*
- *seeking additional resources.*
- *determining the usefulness and accuracy of their information.*
- *putting information together in a meaningful and effective way.*

The instructors—teacher, technology coordinator, and library media specialist—work as a team and help students to problem solve what they want to accomplish. Much of their assistance is in the form of questions such as, "Could you go over exactly what you did?" "Where did you encounter a problem?" "What are some other ways you might attack this problem?" Students spend time in brief, on-the-fly conferences with their instructors. Students also compose short entries in their "thinking journals" to reflect on these problems. In addition, they consult with other student teams that might be experiencing similar difficulties.

The teacher regularly brings the teams together to debrief and to focus their attention on a large class matrix being developed about the changes during the colonial period and their probable causes.

What can we extract from the above scenario? Several characteristics of an inquiry-based environment emerge:

Questioning is at the center of the learning experience.

Inquiry inspires an excitement for learning. In the scenario presented, the unit itself is framed by an essential or big question. With the help of their instructors, students also create more specific questions that are related to their own research projects. As they collect information, they are encouraged to generate more questions that provoke deeper levels of understanding. As they stumble and hit roadblocks, instructors guide students to think through their problems by asking additional questions about strategies used and new options to try.

Students help to negotiate the direction of the learning.

Instructors practice the art of guidance and facilitation as they work with students. While direct teaching is still a valued part of the overall learning experience, instructors spend more time listening to and observing what students do and asking questions that give them further insight into what students actually know. Through this process, students realize the legitimacy of what they want to know and gain confidence in finding their own answers to questions.

Learning is social and interactive.

Students work in groups. The teacher teams with colleagues on the staff. The synergy of these exchanges brings substance and richness to the entire learning discourse. By working cooperatively and collaboratively, people often discover creative solutions to difficult situations and develop respect for diverse perspectives on a topic or an issue.

Solving problems is an integral part of the process.

The ability to recognize problems and to devise strategies to confront them is an essential life skill for students. They need to challenge themselves with questions such as, "Why didn't this work?" "What can I do next?" Being able to apply systematic reasoning strengthens students' abilities to distinguish causes from the symptoms of problems. It also fosters a reexamination of alternative strategies to resolve problems.

Students learn by doing.

The spectrum of activities in a unit or a project reflects both physical and intellectual engagement, i.e., what some educators call hands-on and minds-on interaction. Students in the fifth grade scenario are using the tools of a historian when they examine primary documents to support their findings. They perform tasks that require higher order thinking as they formulate questions, identify steps in completing their projects, and implement their action plans. Some activities are overt, i.e., the students are constructing things or doing live demonstrations. Other activities that deal more centrally with the students' thinking processes are not as directly observable. However, students can prepare journal entries that describe their thinking. Instructors can also confer with students to better understand the rationale and motivation behind a student's actions.

Products and performances reflect application and transfer of learning.

In their products, students not only demonstrate what they understand from their readings, discussions, and observations; they also display how they can transfer this learning to another situation. For example, in the scenario presented students created a "fifth grade compact." To do this successfully, they had to first understand the basic premises of a compact such as the one devised by the Mayflower colonists. By applying their understanding, students exhibited the depth of their own newly acquired knowledge.

Learning is authentic.

The learning experiences are linked to students' personal lives or they are connected to larger social issues. Importantly, students' products and performances are intended for audiences other than the teacher. The students wrestle with questions such as, "How does this influence my own life?" "Why does this matter in today's world?" "How can I share what I know with other people?" In short, students come to realize that what they are learning truly matters. They discover a purpose for learning and for communicating that learning. To move students from fact-centered questions to these types of questions requires continuous modeling and thinking aloud with students. They need to see and to discuss the levels of questioning possible.

Assessment is continuous.

Assessment is done continuously and by both instructors and students. It can take many forms including observations, conferences, graphic organizers, and journals. Importantly, the tools selected for assessment must clearly address the learning outcomes desired. The critical questions to ask in determining assessment measures are: What do we expect students to demonstrate? How might we best measure this performance?

How Does an Inquiry-Based Learning Environment Differ from a Conventional One?

Numerous educational leaders, among them Perkins (1992, 1991) and Wiggins and McTighe (1998), have identified the attributes of high quality schools. They concur that schools which produce stimulating learning communities offer learning experiences that blend knowledge, skills and thinking processes. Figure 1.1 profiles the distinguishing characteristics of inquiry-focused schools contrasted with those of conventional schools:

Figure 1.1: Comparison of Conventional and Inquiry-Focused Schools

Attributes	Conventional school	Inquiry-focused school
Students	Passive learners	Active, engaged learners
Teachers, library media specialists	Content-oriented Teacher as information provider	Student-oriented Teacher as facilitator
Scheduling	Rigid	Flexible
School culture	Bureaucratic	Collaborative
Curriculum and instruction	Textbook-driven Teacher-focused Breadth emphasized Topic-oriented Fragmented	Standards-driven Student-negotiated Depth emphasized Thematic or problem-based Integrated
Assessment	Evaluation at the end Right answers are stressed Teacher assesses Grading is the goal Asks, "what do we know?"	Assessment is ongoing Diverse responses are encouraged Students and teacher assess Goal is improving learning and teaching Asks, "how do we come to know?"
Resources	Restricted to resources available in the classroom	Expands to resources beyond the school
Technology	Focus on learning about technology	Use of technology as a tool for learning

We can now use the characteristics of an inquiry-focused school that have been identified in Figure 1.1 to analyze the fifth grade scenario presented earlier (see Figure 1.2).

Figure 1.2: Analysis of Fifth Grade Unit According to Characteristics of an Inquiry-Focused School

Attributes	Inquiry-focused school	Fifth grade example
Students	Active, engaged learners	Students work in teams to solve problems, conduct research, and communicate findings.
Teachers, library media specialists	Student-oriented	Instructors practice active listening, facilitative questioning, close observation to guide rather than direct students.
Scheduling	Flexible	Students move between classroom, library media center, and computer lab as needed.
School culture	Collaborative	Teacher, library media specialist, and technology coordinator work as a team in planning and co-teaching the unit.
Curriculum and instruction	Standards-driven Student-negotiated Depth emphasized Thematic or problem-based Integrated	The colonization unit is thematic and based on content standards. Students select specific focuses for their research and choose the formats for their final presentations. The overarching question demands deeper analysis and synthesis. Social studies, language arts, fine arts, and information literacy are integrated in this unit.
Assessment	Students and teachers assess Diverse responses are encouraged Goal is improving learning and teaching Assessment is ongoing	Students keep journals throughout the project. Instructors continually monitor student progress. Instructors encourage thinking and actions that reflect independent but thoughtful responses. Assessment informs changes to teaching and learning strategies.

The most telling difference between the inquiry-focused school and other schools is a profound shift in emphasis from textbook-dictated teaching to student-focused learning. Faculties start to ask, "How do students learn?" "Do we encourage students to formulate their own ideas based on data they collect?" "Do we foster the transfer of learning to new and different situations?" "Do we have extended conversations with students regarding their learning?" "Do we encourage such conversations among students?" "Are students relating their learning to the real world?

In inquiry environments, students demonstrate understanding as they explain how something works, interpret the meaning of text, give examples or analogies to clarify ideas, show how things are alike and different, and develop generalizations based upon facts (Unger, 2002; Newmann & Wehlage, 1993; Perkins, 1991). These and other performances provoke learners to strive for deeper levels of comprehension.

How Do We Create an Inquiry-Based Learning Environment?

Creating an environment that supports inquiry begins with the school community's consensus that its mission is developing students who are critical thinkers and problem solvers. While most schools would hardly argue that this is a central goal for them, building a school culture in which such learning actually occurs requires a hard-nosed examination of actual practices.

Wehlage (1999) in his evaluation of Library Power schools, indicated the dilemma and disconnect between mission and actual school practices. Our work with schools in our own state and in other states corroborates the observations below:

- Students work independently more often than they do in teams.
- Inquiry as a process of learning is not clearly evident in practice (e.g., hands-on activities may not be connected to analysis or building evidence).
- The lion's share of the annual school budget is spent on textbooks and workbooks. At the same time, the library media center budget is dwindling.
- Professional development is conducted largely as one-shot efforts with limited, if any, follow-through during the school year.
- Technology training usually focuses on the technical aspects of using software programs rather than the learning implications of technology use.
- Classroom teachers lean heavily on evaluation at the end rather than ongoing assessment. Quizzes and tests remain the norm.
- Staff time for collaborative planning is minimal and incidental. There is no training for working effectively in collaborative groups.
- Professional development focuses on separate strands for teachers and for library media specialists.

To effect real change, a school community must wrestle with the following essential questions:

- What should students learn?
- How should students learn?
- How should learning be assessed?
- How might technology support learning?
- What interactions and relationships enhance learning?
- How can we promote continuous school-wide improvement?

In Figure 1.3, we suggest how a school might respond to these questions and the types of action strategies that lead to substantive change.

Figure 1.3: Building an Inquiry-Based Environment: Examples of Action Strategies

Essential questions	Possible action strategies
What should students learn?	Conduct retreats to shape school's overall vision and mission. Establish articulation committees across departments or grade levels to build curriculum around big ideas that connect to the real world. Focus on thinking processes as well as content knowledge and skills.
How should students learn?	Build professional development opportunities to design learning environments that promote investigation, higher level questioning, and hands-on activities that lead to understanding.
How should learning be assessed?	Build professional development opportunities to clarify learning outcomes and design measurements that help to assess outcomes.
How might technology support learning?	Build professional development opportunities to integrate technology into learning experiences.
What interactions and relationships enhance learning?	Emphasize collaborative partnerships. For example, provide quarterly planning time for grade level or departmental curriculum planning.
How might continuous school-wide improvement be promoted?	Provide administrative leadership in establishing a comprehensive school improvement plan. Use the plan to guide the school in achieving its goals. Involve key stakeholders as members of various committees working on different facets of the plan.

What Role Does the Library Media Program Play?

Information Power: Building Partnerships for Learning (AASL & AECT, 1998) challenges library media specialists to rethink their roles as teachers and as instructional partners. Harada (2003) contends that library media specialists are strategically positioned to work with entire school populations and to examine curriculum from a big picture perspective.

In an inquiry-based school, library media specialists are key team members in identifying the skills and habits of mind that nurture thinking in the various disciplines and in the development of information literacy. They can assist their school teams in making the following types of connections (Dalbotten, 1997):

- In history, students formulate questions, obtain data from both primary and secondary sources, evaluate the information in terms of its accuracy and authority, and identify propaganda or distortion. They analyze their data and construct arguments or summarize findings. Assessment is built in to their ongoing work.
- In science, students create testable hypotheses, design and conduct experiments and investigations, revise explanations using logic and evidence, and communicate and defend their results. They assess their progress and evaluate their final product.
- In the information search process, students identify their information need, generate questions that further define the need, devise strategies to locate and retrieve relevant information, evaluate and organize findings, and communicate what they learn. They continually examine what they are learning and how they are learning it.

Whether it is a historical study, a scientific investigation, or an information problem, there are similar thinking skills and dispositions reflected in all of these processes. The thinking skills involve:

- Recognition and articulation of a problem or an issue.
- Location and critical retrieval of information to investigate the problem or issue.
- Organization and synthesis of collected information.
- Interpretation, analysis, and use of information.
- Preparation and communication of newly acquired knowledge.
- Ongoing assessment and evaluation of work.

Figure 1.4 presents one example of how thinking skills might be aligned with what students learn in the classroom and the library media center.

As students progress through the information search process, they pose questions and gather information needed to solve problems. As one question is probed, others present themselves, leading students into more complex layers of knowledge. The effectiveness of the process lies in a student's ability to manipulate the information so that deeper levels of personal understanding are achieved.

Figure 1.4: Example of Aligning Thinking Skills and Attitudes with Learning in the Classroom and Literacy Media Center

Thinking skills/attitudes	Classroom	Library media center
Be curious and explore.	Explore a general topic: view videos and TV, talk to people, go on field trips, engage in class discussions.	Explore a general topic: browse shelves and Internet sites.
Recognize and articulate a problem or issue.	Formulate a focus for project: create webs, confer with others, generate questions.	⟹
Plan and be strategic. Identify how learning will be assessed.	Plan the project: set goals, identify tasks, and assign responsibilities and deadlines.	Plan search strategies.
Retrieve and evaluate information. Organize and synthesize information.	Collect relevant information: emphasize accuracy of information and authority of sources.	Collect relevant information: set criteria for good notes, use multiple resources, use graphic organizers, and cite sources.
Interpret, analyze, and use information. Build explanations and understandings.	Analyze data. Construct arguments or summarize findings.	Evaluate information: examine collected information, generate more questions, and seek additional information.
Prepare and communicate newly acquired knowledge.	Prepare and present: clarify purpose, identify audience, select presentation form, draft, revise, rehearse.	⟹
Assess and evaluate product and process.	Reflect: design assessment tools; conduct self, peer, and instructor assessments.	⟹

Conclusion

Information skills are among the basic skills students need to succeed in this century (Marzano, 2001; North Central Regional Educational Laboratory, n.d.). If students are to be adventurous thinkers, they need access to resources that will extend their thinking and suggest new paths to knowledge. To be problem finders and investigators, they must experience and reflect on the diverse problems that exist in the world. They must learn reading and research strategies that enable them to interpret complex ideas.

In an inquiry environment, the library media center is more than a physical collection of resources. It is a place where questions can be raised and problems posed. It is a portal to the knowledge banks of the world. It is a learning center where students develop the skills to manage an ever-increasing volume of information. The library media center is the epicenter, the heartbeat, of the school.

2 Describing an Inquiry-Driven Curriculum

This chapter:
- Describes the importance of questions that drive inquiry.
- Examines how critical thinking and problem solving skills are reflected in inquiry learning.
- Explains the place of standards in relation to an inquiry approach.
- Suggests the function of the library media center in promoting inquiry.

What Is Involved in Inquiry Learning?

Inquiry learning is more than asking questions and looking for answers (Exline, n.d.). It is an approach to learning that involves students in a spiraling cycle of questioning, investigating, verifying, and generating new questions. As one student wrote in her reflection journal: "You can never get to the bottom of it. As soon as you think you've found an answer, another question pops up!"

Pappas and Tepe (2002) describe inquiry learning as "an investigative process that engages students in answering questions, solving real world problems, confronting issues, or exploring personal interests" (p. 27). It involves exploring the world, making discoveries, and rigorously testing those discoveries in search of new understanding (Center for Research on Learning and Technology at Indiana University, 1999-2000). In short, inquiry learning is a dynamic process that uses questioning to actively involve students in their own learning.

Why Use an Inquiry Approach to Teaching and Learning?

Inquiry forms the bedrock of an effective student-based school curriculum. What differentiates inquiry learning from other instructional approaches is the emphasis on questioning, investigation, and experimentation. Students who learn in this way are actively involved in creating new knowledge and developing deeper levels of understanding.

Inquiry-driven instruction takes advantage of children's natural curiosity. It builds on their innate instincts towards discovery and observation. It involves students in decisions about what will be learned, how learning will take place, and how success will be measured. Inquiry makes learning relevant by providing a context that gives purpose to the tasks involved.

The benefits of inquiry apply to everyone in the school setting:

- Students benefit when they are given opportunities to pursue their own interests or problems of their choosing. They develop the skills of observation, questioning, critical thinking, and problem solving. Once acquired, these skills can be applied in countless other situations.

- Teachers benefit from working in close collaboration with other members of the school team. They are invigorated professionally and personally when there is a collegial atmosphere.
- The library media specialist and technology coordinator benefit when the school values the contributions of each support program in curriculum development.
- Parents benefit when the school has a consistent approach to instructional delivery that welcomes the active participation of parents.
- School administrators benefit when the curriculum provides a vehicle for addressing school-wide goals and achieving standards, many of which involve elements of inquiry.

How Are Essential and Unit Questions Used to Focus the Inquiry?

The essential question is an effective means of organizing the inquiry process (Kuhlthau, 1993; Cushman, 1989). According to Wiggins and McTighe (1998) essential questions "engage students in uncovering the important ideas at the heart of each subject" (p. 28). They may be used to frame a unit of study or even an entire course.

Essential questions are used to move instruction away from a succession of activities suggested by the topic to a focus on important ideas and major issues. The following questions are examples of essential questions that have been used to organize instructional units:

- What do living things need to survive?
- Why is water important?
- How has the earth changed over time?
- How does the Bill of Rights affect your life today?
- How does conflict cause literary characters to grow and change?
- What does art reveal about a culture?

As these examples illustrate, essential questions share the following characteristics:

- They are open-ended.
- They are global and abstract in nature.
- They go to the heart of the discipline—pointing out what is really important to learn.
- They lead to the enduring truths that students will remember long after the facts have been forgotten.
- They are asked over and over throughout the course of study.
- They lead to other important questions, problems, and issues.

Because they are abstract and global, essential questions alone may be too broad to effectively guide student inquiry. Hence, there is a need to break them down to teachable questions, i.e., unit questions.

Unit questions have a different function from essential questions. Although they always point to the essential questions, they are more closely connected to a particular topic, problem, or issue. Their purpose is to let students know more precisely what they are responsible for learning. Like essential questions, unit questions are often open-ended, allowing for many different interpretations, explanations, and solutions.

Essential and unit questions work in harmony. In designing a unit, the planners must first decide upon the "big" ideas they want students to take from the study. These ideas are used to formulate essential questions. The next step is to write questions for the unit of study that will connect with the essential question and help students to interpret it. Figure 2.1 shows how essential questions generate more specific unit questions.

Figure 2.1: Examples of Essential and Unit Questions

Essential questions	Unit questions
How has racism affected the history and culture of the United States?	• What examples of racism exist in the United States? • What events in U. S. history can be directly linked to racism? • How does the United States Constitution deal with the issue of racism?
Why is conflict important in a story?	• What conflicts does Julie face in *Julie of the Wolves*? • How does Julie change as a result of conflict? • What is the relationship between the conflict and the story setting?

What Might Essential and Unit Questions Look Like in Practice?

Let's take a closer look at how the use of essential and unit questions shaped the social studies curriculum for one group of fifth grade teachers and students. The teachers looked for a theme that encompassed United States history from the Age of Exploration through the Westward Movement. They decided upon the theme of change because they wanted students to understand history as a succession of causes and effects.

The teachers identified three units of instruction dealing with variations on the theme of change. The essential question was, "How has the United States changed over time?" Figure 2.2 shows how unit questions were generated from the essential question. It also includes more specific questions contributed by the students.

Figure 2.2: Using Essential and Unit Questions to Guide Student Inquiry

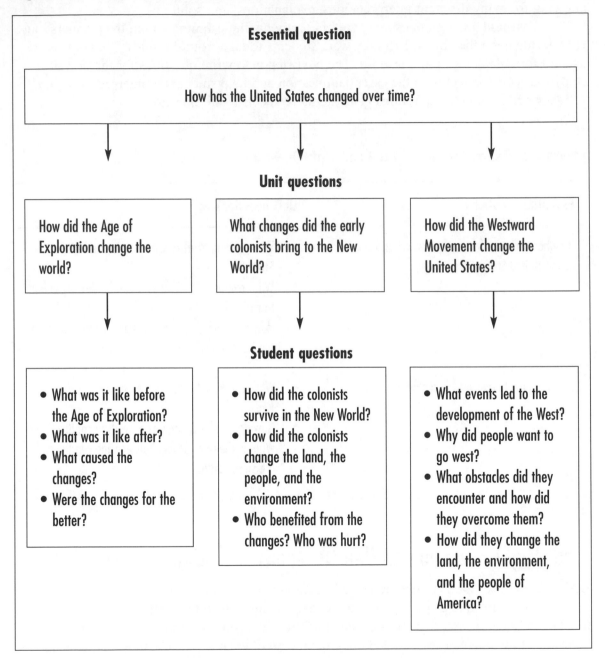

Once the essential and unit questions were developed and students brainstormed their additional questions, the following sequence of activities was initiated:

- Students collected, analyzed, and synthesized information.
- Teachers referred students back to the essential questions as new understandings were discovered.
- Students developed increasingly complex levels of understanding as they probed the big questions and planned their presentations.

- Different viewpoints began to emerge as students discussed their findings. Differences in interpretation led to additional questions followed by a refocused quest for information.
- Students reflected on what they were learning, how they were learning, and the difficulties they were having with both the process and their final presentations. Teachers used these reflections to modify the process and provide guidance to individuals and groups.

In this yearlong study, students engaged in a series of mini-projects that ranged from writing expository essays about the impact of exploration on the New World to devising board games on the Westward Movement. Students became colonists and demonstrated how the skills and trades of these first European settlers influenced our way of life. They assumed the viewpoints of different people who ventured to the West and composed letters to folks back home about what life was like, the obstacles they faced, and how their achievements were helping America grow. Besides staging a culminating history fair of the students' best products, students and teachers constructed wall webs that captured how key events related to each other in these three important periods of U.S. history and how they impacted the growth of our nation. Through it all, teachers facilitated continuous attention on the essential and unit questions. At the end, one teacher commented as follows:

> At first I thought the big question was just something you put up on the board at the beginning and went back to at the end of the unit. But this time, I used the questions throughout the unit to keep the class focused on big ideas rather than bits and pieces of information. For example, when students found information about the obstacles encountered by pioneers and how they dealt with them, the students wrote about this on a chart. A few times each week we would review the chart and relate the information to the unit question and the essential question about change. The big questions provided an anchor for the unit. It is so easy to get lost in a sea of facts and fail to get at the important understandings. This is one idea that works in the classroom!

What Attitudes or Habits of Mind Are Developed?

In chapter 1 we described the critical thinking skills practiced by students in an inquiry-focused environment. The inquiry-based curriculum places thinking at the top of the list of teaching priorities. However, as many educators have pointed out, good thinkers possess more than skills. They have the ability and the inclination to use those skills appropriately in a given situation. These intellectual traits, often referred to as thinking dispositions or habits of mind, (Perkins, 1992; Tishman & Andrade, 1999; Ennis, 2002) are critical to successful inquiry.

The work done at Harvard's Project Zero (Perkins, 1992; Tishman & Andrade, 1999) indicates that children learn to think when there is a culture of thinking in the classroom. Creating such a culture cannot be left to chance. Educators need to deliberately create environments that support attitudes and behaviors that encourage higher levels of thinking. Various researchers have identified clusters of desirable thinking dispositions (Ennis, 2002; Tishman & Andrade, 1999; Wiggins & McTighe, 1998; Facione, Sanchez, Facione, &

Gainen, 1995; Perkins, 1992). From their works, we selected the following skills and attitudes as most essential for inquiry learning.

Curiosity and inquisitiveness

Inquiry is not a "one right answer" approach to learning. Students ask questions beginning with "how" and "why" as well as "who" and "what." They engage in a cycle of learning that involves locating, analyzing, organizing, and synthesizing information from multiple resources and diverse fields of knowledge. They reflect on their findings and generate additional questions in a continuous quest for deeper understanding.

Truth seeking

Inquiry is, above all, a search for explanations that must be pursued and validated. Inquiry instruction encourages students to question the obvious and to seek answers through experimentation and investigation. Accuracy in terms of the information gathered and the integrity of the investigative process are primary concerns in an inquiry environment. Assessment criteria at each stage in the process must reflect the need for accuracy and truth.

Sustained intellectual activity

Inquiry learning involves students in an investigative process that takes them deeply into a problem or an issue in a search for explanations and reasons. The goal is not to find an answer but to uncover layers of knowledge and, ultimately, deeper levels of understanding. Clarification is sought through investigation and exhaustive research. All findings are subject to validation. The inquiry never comes to an end as each layer of knowledge presents new inquiries. Because value is placed on the process of constructing knowledge, students learn the rewards of engaging in high levels of intellectual activity over an extended period of time.

Thoughtful planning

Inquiry involves many different skills, processes, and practical considerations. Students need to know how to proceed with an inquiry by making a plan of action and learning how to follow it. Checklists and other guides can help students to follow a strategic plan. The goal is for students to learn how to develop their own action plans and to use them to monitor their progress.

Reflection and self-monitoring

Students need to weigh evidence, consider options, and make conscious choices about how to approach problems and issues. Decisions are the result of deliberate thinking and informed problem solving. Metacognition is vital to inquiry learning. Throughout the process students reflect on what they are doing, how they are learning, and the problems they are having.

Open-mindedness

As students gather information to answer their questions, the evidence often generates additional questions. These questions may point the researcher in another direction or cause him to rethink the original hypothesis. Students need to be open-minded in their interpretation of the evidence and flexible in adjusting their strategies.

Where Do Content Standards Fit In?

Most states and school districts have implemented two types of standards:

Types of standards

Content standards: These are goals of learning. They specify what students should know and be able to do in each area of the curriculum. Since these standards are fixed, student performance is measured against the standard instead of against the performance of other students.

Performance standards: These tell what a student product or performance looks like if it meets the standard. They describe levels of performance and the kinds of evidence needed to show that content standards have been met. Performance standards are measured by looking at student work and judging it in terms of the content standard (Mitchell, 1995).

Content standards from various disciplines directly relate to inquiry learning. For example, in language arts students "must conduct research on issues and interests by generating ideas and questions, and by posing problems" (National Council of Teachers of English and International Reading Association, n.d.). In science, students must develop "the abilities necessary to do scientific inquiry" and the "understandings about scientific inquiry" (National Academy of Sciences, n.d.). In mathematics, students must "apply and adapt a variety of appropriate strategies to solve problems," to "develop and evaluate arguments and proofs," and to "communicate their mathematical thinking coherently and clearly to peers" (National Council of Teachers of Mathematics, 2000).

These types of content standards make inquiry the primary learning target. Linked to these content standards are the performance standards that describe how students demonstrate whether or not they have achieved the targeted goals.

Some practical advice—target just a few key standards for each project. The goal of inquiry learning is depth, not breadth. Students need time to observe, to discuss, to question, and to investigate. To rush the process is to short-change the students.

How Does the Library Media Program Support Inquiry Learning?

The library media center provides a natural environment for inquiry (AASL & AECT, 1998). Fundamental to inquiry learning is information seeking and information use. Students ask questions, gather facts and data, analyze and evaluate information, and present findings to an audience. Whether the subject matter is science, history, art, or archaeology, the student is engaged in a quest for knowledge.

Figure 2.3 captures how the library media specialist supports inquiry by providing the resources, the instructional support, and the ease of access needed for students to pursue meaningful knowledge and to apply critical thinking and problem solving skills.

Figure 2.3: How Library Media Specialists Support Inquiry

Function	Supporting inquiry learning
Teaching and learning	• Actively teach the information search process. • Invite and facilitate thoughtful questioning. • Model how to access, evaluate, and use information. • Promote continual assessment.
Physical environment	• Arrange spaces for multiple groupings. • Allow for flexible scheduling. • Provide for easy and safe access.
Resources	• Provide access to a range of resources in a variety of formats. • Provide resources to meet diverse needs. • Enable electronic access to global resources.
Building learning communities	• Play key role in creating learning communities that link students and teachers with human and information resources beyond the school.

Conclusion

Questions are central to inquiry. As library media specialists and teachers, the challenge is to help students realize that the quality of the questions they generate ultimately determines the quality of the investigations they conduct.

A word of advice for those planning an inquiry project for the first time—be patient with yourself and with your students. Resist the temptation to overwhelm students with a catalog of facts and a list of activities to be completed. Instead, allow time for discovery, exploration, and observation. Encourage questions. Present models. Interact with your students and colleagues. And, most importantly, provide direction, encouragement, and guidance.

3 Developing Collaborative Relationships

Everyone wins when teachers and library media specialists collaborate with other staff members on instruction. For schools engaged in inquiry-based learning, collaboration is more than an added bonus; it is the life force behind such instruction.

> **This chapter:**
> - Describes factors that contribute to collaborative relationships.
> - Identifies skills and attitudes necessary to collaborate.
> - Suggests strategies to get started.

If the goal of inquiry is to involve students in authentic learning experiences and higher level thinking processes, collaboration is indispensable. Every member of the instructional team must be involved in helping students to acquire the content, skills, and habits of thinking that are involved in inquiry learning. Teachers, library media specialists, technology coordinators, and other school staff must work together to set goals, plan learning experiences, instruct students, and assess learning. Importantly, students are also part of the collaborative planning process.

Why should busy classroom teachers want to participate in such a process? Effective partnerships help teachers to meet their existing priorities, which include the implementation of a standards-based curriculum. Such partnerships have the following benefits:

- Access to a range of resources for both teacher and student.
- Support in using various technologies for learning and teaching.
- Opportunities for creative synergy and collegial problem solving.

Why is the library media specialist such a potentially powerful member in a collaborative team? The ability to construct meaning is at the heart of information literacy. By helping students master information literacy—which is essential to mastering curricular content, critical thinking, and problem solving—the library media program makes a unique contribution to their learning. There is ample research to support the idea that authentic learning and information literacy have a symbiotic relationship Gross & Kientz, 1999; Kuhlthau, 1995). Russell (2000) further indicates that students are more apt to acquire the complex skills needed to cope with the increasing volume of information in a collaborative culture.

In short, information skills cannot be taught separately from the thinking processes that are needed to master content. Nor can teachers provide an authentic curriculum, grounded in real-world experiences, without the inclusion of information skills in the instructional plan. If collaboration is a necessity in today's workplace—and we want our students to practice this—we must model the same behavior (Bush, 2003).

What Does Collaboration Look Like?

Grover (1996) describes collaboration as a working relationship that is developed over a relatively long period of time. As the relationship evolves, participants negotiate shared goals, clearly define their roles, and work on comprehensive planning (Haycock cited in Kearney, 2000).

The following scenario provides an example of how collaborative relationships impact an inquiry-focused project:

> *At Aloha Middle School students are divided into interdisciplinary groups. An instructional team that is comprised of language arts, social studies, mathematics, and science teachers guides each group. Teaching teams meet with the library media specialist, technology coordinator, and other support staff to develop inquiry-based units of learning during days set aside for professional development. At these planning sessions the teams discuss their mutual goals, map out curriculum, and decide on the instructional focus for their respective projects.*
>
> *One team organizes its curriculum around the essential question, "How does conflict affect life in Hawaii?" In social studies, students research historical events in Hawaiian history. Science classes examine conflicts surrounding environmental issues such as the preservation of native ecosystems. Math classes use statistics and probability to predict the effects of population pressure and discuss the resulting problems. Finally, the language arts classes focus on strengthening reading and writing skills that students need to critically think about and to communicate their findings in social studies, science, and math.*
>
> *Throughout the process, students help with decisions about what to learn and how to assess the learning. The library media specialist provides resources and instruction on the information search process. She also actively participates in planning, teaching, and assessing student progress. The technology coordinator—in addition to providing technical support—also works with students on their culminating products. Both the library and computer lab operate on flexible schedules. The administrator supports ongoing collaboration by providing regularly scheduled articulation time for sharing, problem solving, and continued planning.*

What Factors Make Collaboration Work?

Let's analyze and expand upon the scenario just presented. It is apparent that a culture of collaboration exists at Aloha Middle School. People from different fields working together define this culture. They reach decisions through consensus. Students and staff members participate in setting goals, planning activities, and assessing achievement. The commitment appears to be long-standing and focused on long-term results. Planning is continuous, rather than a one-time event. Faculty and administration share a common goal: to create a learning environment that enables all students to master the content, skills, and processes that lead to meaningful learning.

This is a far cry from the traditional school where the norm is not consensus building, but competition for power based on personal agendas. Rather than focusing on short-term activities and programs, the school community envisions larger results and develops strategies to achieve them (Grover, 1996).

Figure 3.1 summarizes some of the school-wide factors that are essential for effective collaboration.

Figure 3.1: School-Wide Factors That Support Collaboration

Factors	Commentary
Culture of collaboration	There is a shared vision in the school. Faculty members have common goals. They work in teams. Curriculum planning and assessment are ongoing activities. Students are involved in the process.
Scheduling and library access	The library media center and computer lab operate on either a flexible or a modified instruction schedule that allows for student use on a timely basis. Teachers and students have ready access to both facilities.
Administrative support	Administration supports collaboration with scheduled planning time, professional development, and resources.
Access to information resources	The library media center provides access to a range of appropriate resources in various formats. It also connects the school with current information available in the community and on the Internet.

What Skills and Attitudes Do People Need to Collaborate?

Beyond issues such as scheduling and access to resources, collaboration depends on positive human interactions that influence people's willingness to work together. Collaboration is a complex process that requires participants to change their perceptions, attitudes, and expectations (Muronaga & Harada, 1999; Wolcott, 1996). These less tangible aspects ultimately determine the success of the collaborative effort. Several key elements are discussed below under the headings of communication and group planning and management.

Communication

In planning sessions, we use both verbal and nonverbal cues to communicate our messages (Friend & Cook, 2000). Figure 3.2 identifies several types of verbal cues and provides examples of these cues in action from a library media specialist's perspective.

Figure 3.2: Verbal cues

Verbal Cues	Cues in Action
Encourage explanation.	A teacher mentions that she is unhappy with the last set of student reports. You ask, "What were students unable to do well?"
Suspend judgment.	A teacher suggests that students start their search with the Internet. You personally think they should start with print resources but instead of saying this, you offer, "Let's do a trial run and see how the Internet might work."
Avoid unsolicited advice.	A teacher mentions in the lunchroom that one of his students is a disciplinary problem in his class. He is not seeking advice but simply venting. You have seen the student in your library but you don't know her well. You avoid commenting on the situation.
Provide specific feedback.	A team of teachers is working with you on a unit dealing with beautifying the school campus. The teachers are stymied regarding resources that students might use for their research on the topic. You suggest resources on the Internet and in the community that can be tapped for specific areas of study on this larger issue.
Confirm or clarify information received.	You are working with a team that is designing a unit on endangered local plants. The project involves both social studies and science teachers. There is some confusion about the standards being addressed. You offer the following: "We seem to have at least two possible standards in the area of science that this unit directly addresses. What we don't seem to have yet is a social studies standard. Do you agree?"

Equally important, and subtler, are nonverbal signals that accompany our verbal messages. Figure 3.3 categorizes these cues and presents some positive demonstrations of these cues.

Figure 3.3: Nonverbal cues

Nonverbal Cues	Cues in Action
Body movements such as facial expression, eye contact, posture, and gesture.	Smile and nod approval as appropriate; make direct eye contact; lean toward rather than away from speakers.
Quality of voice, volume, and pacing of speech.	Make sure that you can be heard; speak clearly and pace your speech so that others can follow your train of thought.
Physical distance between participants.	Configure the meeting space so that people can see and hear each other and have room to work.

Group planning and management

The library media specialist often assumes the lead in a collaborative relationship (Buzzeo, 2002; AASL & AECT, 1998; Grover, 1996). This necessitates skills in facilitating group meetings.

Several tips in handling these sessions include the following (Bush, 2003; Muronaga & Harada, 1999):

- Set measurable and realistic goals for the meeting.
- Clearly state these goals up front.
- Succinctly recap the results of the previous meeting and how today's goals build on prior work.
- Encourage everyone to participate.
- Facilitate but do not dominate the conversation.
- Avoid monopolization of conversation by vocal team members.
- Use positive verbal and nonverbal cues to keep the exchanges constructive and targeted.
- Continually summarize the exchanges and focus the group on the session's goals.
- Respect differences in opinions but at the same time guide the group in seeking consensus. Look for areas where agreements are possible.
- At the end of the session, debrief on whether or not the meeting's goals were met.
- Recap tasks and responsibilities that team members have agreed upon.
- Set next meeting date and place.
- Take simple minutes of the meeting and disseminate it to all participants.

Team members bring a range of expertise to the table including knowledge and skills in different content areas, teaching strategies, and methods for assessing learning outcomes. The notion of shared participation, therefore, is crucial. This does not mean that tasks must be equally divided amongst the team; however, everyone must be equally involved in the decisions made. In addition, each member must have resources to contribute. The degree and nature of the contributions would depend on the situation and the specific activity (Muronaga & Harada, 1999). Figure 3.4 illustrates this concept.

Because inquiry learning also requires that students be involved in the ongoing assessment for learning, the team must be ready to make adjustments. Figure 3.5 captures the flexible, nonlinear nature of the interaction.

Figure 3.4: Example of Shared Participation

Situation

A team comprised of a fifth grade teacher, the technology coordinator, and the library media specialist collaborate on a unit that compares celebrations in countries around the world. Working in teams, students select a type of celebration found in at least two countries (e.g., a harvest celebration). They investigate the celebration and produce illustrations and text for a class book that will be donated to the library. The table below outlines the responsibilities of the three instructors.

Responsibilities

The classroom teacher:	The library media specialist:	The technology coordinator:
Mr. A's expertise is in social studies. Having done this unit before, he is comfortable with both content and assessment of learning outcomes. He introduces the study in his classroom and explains the final product. He designs a rubric and involves the other two instructors in assessing drafts of student work.	Mrs. B's expertise is in information literacy skills and access to resources. She teaches students how to locate, retrieve, and evaluate information from print and Internet resources. Because Mr. A is not sure about how to teach note taking, Mrs. B also introduces a mapping activity with the students.	Miss C's expertise is in using technology applications for student productions. She becomes actively involved with the students when they are ready to prepare drafts of their text and illustrations. Students work with her in the computer lab.
He also supports the team throughout the project by following up in the classroom with instruction initiated in the library and computer lab.	She supports the team by assisting with assessment of student work. Students also return to the library in small groups as needed to collect additional information.	She supports the team by assisting with the assessment of student work. She also provides additional guidance in computer-related activities as needed.

Figure 3.5: Example of Flexible Planning

Situation
A team comprised of middle school health education and language arts teachers, the technology coordinator, and the library media specialist collaborate on a unit dealing with nutritional habits of students at their school. Students decide on the following goal: to recommend changes to the snacks being sold by the student council during recesses. To achieve their goal, the students devise and conduct a campus poll and base their recommendations on their library research and the results of the poll.

Original Unit Plan and Adjustments to the Unit		
Original plan	**Assessment**	**Adjustments made**
In health: Spend two sessions introducing topic and having students determine final product.	Journal accounts revealed that students knew less about the general topic of nutrition than the teacher anticipated.	Teacher added two more sessions. Students spent part of the time browsing through resources in the library.
In library: Spend one session searching for a comparable study of nutritional habits.	Observations showed that students were fuzzy about keyword searching.	Library media specialist spent another session on keyword search strategies.
In language arts: Spend two sessions devising questions for the campus poll.	Observation revealed that students had limited prior knowledge about surveys.	Teacher added two sessions where she presented models of surveys.
During lunch and recess: Spend two weeks conducting the poll.	In ongoing progress checks, the team discovered that students were able to gather data more quickly than anticipated.	Students decided to reduce the time from two weeks to one week for the poll.
In health: Spend two sessions summarizing the data from the poll.	Observations indicated that students had different interpretations of data.	Teacher spent another session having students reach consensus on this matter.
In computer lab: Spend two sessions learning how to create effective visual presentations of findings.	Students had difficulty determining how to effectively communicate their messages.	Technology coordinator spent an extra session comparing different modes of display.

In a collaborative setting, planning goes beyond the formal discussions that often take place at the start of a unit or a term. Although this initial planning is essential to create a framework for designing instruction, the inquiry method requires ongoing articulation among the members of the instructional team. Since students are involved in decisions about what will be learned, how learning will take place, and how it will be assessed, teachers and the library media specialist need to engage them in an ongoing dialogue throughout the process.

Because this type of group planning is based on a continuous assessment of student performance, it is also a fluid process. Members must be flexible and ready to make adjustments in their teaching. Figure 3.5 captures the flexible, nonlinear nature of the interaction.

Cooperation and coordination

Bush (2003), Kearney (2000), Grover (1996) and others have found it useful to place the interactions between teachers and library media specialists on a continuum beginning with limited attempts at cooperative planning and moving toward the total involvement of the library media specialist in curriculum planning and implementation. They indicate that fledgling partnerships might involve cooperation or coordination. The gradations between coordination, cooperation, and collaboration are outlined in Figure 3.6. We also present scenarios that describe situations where coordination and cooperation are evident and suggest how to build toward collaboration from these starting points.

Figure 3.6: Continuum of Teacher and Librarian Partnerships

Cooperation ⟶	Coordination ⟶	Collaboration
Short term	Longer term	Long term commitment
Informal	Some formality	Ongoing relationship
No defined goals	Goals may differ	Clearly defined common goals
Plan independently	Some joint planning	In-depth planning
Teach separately	Sharing of resources	Joint responsibility for student learning
Retain autonomy	Some competition	Power sharing

Cooperative activities stem from informal exchanges. Doiron (cited in Kearney, 2000) notes that teachers and library media specialists plan separately but try to combine goals and content to achieve a desired result. Figure 3.7 provides a scenario involving cooperation.

In this scenario the teacher and the library media specialist have an informal arrangement on a limited basis to implement a topic-based instructional unit. Both partners are using "birds" as content; however, there is little effort to actually plan, teach, or assess together. Although the library media specialist sees an opportunity to teach students about

Figure 3.7: Scenario Involving Cooperation

Over lunch in the teachers' lounge Mrs. Brown mentions that she is planning a unit on birds for her third grade class. Ms. Edwards, the library media specialist, offers to collect fiction and nonfiction books about birds for the children to read in the classroom. She also decides to use the topic of birds as a springboard for a lesson on using the electronic encyclopedia. When Mrs. Brown assigns each of her students to write a brief report on one type of bird, Ms. Edwards suggests that the students use their encyclopedia printouts. Because some of the species are not represented in the encyclopedia, she also introduces a Web site on birds of the world. When the reports are finished, Ms. Edwards offers to display them in the library.

the electronic encyclopedia and the Internet, it is not clear that the teacher realizes that students could practice a process approach to research. Teaching is done independently. Some people refer to this as parallel teaching since goals are separately conceived and executed.

Nonetheless, this is a hopeful beginning for both partners. The students learn to locate, retrieve, and evaluate information from electronic and online resources. The teacher is now aware of resources beyond her classroom. The library media specialist has taken the initiative to provide both resources and instruction without overwhelming the teacher. She has also offered to display the finished products.

The library media specialist has fostered a relationship that might lead to the following options in a future project:

- Suggest a way to introduce an essential question that might frame a unit. This would move it in the direction of an inquiry-focused project.
- Introduce a simple checklist that outlines the research process. She could then suggest skills that she might help teach.

Whereas cooperation is largely informal, coordination involves some advance planning. Figure 3.8 describes an example of this.

Figure 3.8: Scenario Involving Coordination

At Pacific High School, language arts teachers focus on a major author-study project in senior English classes that extends through the second quarter of the school year. The teachers meet during the summer to outline the project. Each student is required to choose an author from an approved list and to write a critique on the author's style based upon at least two of his works. A biographical profile of the author is to be included with the final report. Students must do most of the actual research on their own time. The final report is to be submitted to the teacher for grading.

In the fall, the teachers share this project plan with Mr. Sato, the library media specialist. At that point, the library media specialist suggests that the students might follow a research checklist that he has devised. He also offers to create a pathfinder that students might use to locate information. In addition, he indicates his willingness to teach students the uses of different literary reference works and biographical dictionaries as well as the process of preparing a bibliography.

This scenario reflects coordination between the teachers and the library media specialist. Although the library media specialist has not been involved in the initial development of this project, he has been invited to embellish and expand upon the original plan. The plan itself seems to focus on the mechanics rather than the substance of the project. Do the students possess the prerequisite skills to perform a literary analysis? Do they have an essential question that focuses their analysis? For his part, the library media specialist plans to communicate regularly with teachers to coordinate schedules and to work out problems that may occur with individual students when they visit the library. Teachers will develop assessment criteria for the final product. However, no attempt is being made to assess how well students understand the information search process. The library media specialist will not be involved in ongoing assessment of student work. Nor will he be examining their finished products.

In spite of these shortcomings, there are encouraging signs for future development. For one, teachers in the department are collaborating on curriculum. Although the library media specialist has not been included in the initial and crucial stages of this planning, he has been invited to participate at a later phase. Teachers appear receptive to the library media specialist's various suggestions and they are willing to allow time for library instruction. The library media specialist has volunteered instruction in areas that he is uniquely qualified to teach. Teachers agree that these are critical skills for students to master.

The success of this project might enable the library media specialist to suggest one or more of the following ideas for a similar project next year:

- Express his willingness to join the summer planning group. This would allow for a closer integration of library and classroom goals from the onset.
- Propose that the project introduce a framing question that all students might address in their literary analyses. An example: What makes this author's works so real for us?
- Creating an essential question would focus the inquiry and provoke students to synthesize and to interpret what they have read and experienced.
- Ask if there might be additional audiences for the student work. This might be an opportunity to discuss how students might brainstorm options.
- Volunteer to draft criteria for assessing the information search process. This provides a critical first step in demonstrating the importance of process as well as product evaluation.

How Might We Get Started?

Undisputedly, the road to collaboration is a bumpy one. Many authors, who have written on this topic, acknowledge numerous obstacles (Bush, 2003; Buzzeo, 2002; Small, n.d.; Wolcott, 1994). We have alluded to several of these problems throughout this chapter. They include the following:

- Autonomous working styles of educators.
- Inflexible structure of the school day.
- Textbook-driven curriculum.

- Limited opportunities for collaborative planning during the workday.
- Lack of training in facilitating group work.
- Perceptions of library media specialists as keepers of stored knowledge rather than partners in dynamic learning.

Given these formidable challenges, it would be easy enough to conclude that collaborative relationships are impossible to achieve. We maintain, however, that the stakes are too high for library media specialists to walk away from this challenge. Rather than visualizing these problems as roadblocks, we need to figure out strategies to minimize them and to make them building blocks for nurturing partnerships.

Such partnerships begin with a "conversation between two professionals" (Bush, 2003, p. 92). They can spring from chats in the lunchroom or at a faculty gathering. A vigilant library media specialist can even pick up cues by informally visiting a classroom and quickly observing what is posted around the room.

Although the ultimate goal is to reach deeper levels of joint planning and team teaching that are needed to support inquiry, library media specialists must seize every opportunity to work with teachers and other support staff. This also means adjusting their approach to accommodate others and accepting the fact there is no "right way" to approach planning (Wolcott, 1996, p. 10).

In Figure 3.9 on the following page, we offer examples of partnership-building strategies culled from our own experiences and from suggestions made by other practitioners (Small, 2002; Buzzeo, 2002; Russell, 2000; Logan, 2000). We don't intend that library media specialists perform all of these actions. Instead, we suggest that they start with strategies that are appropriate and doable for their own situations. Remember, these are intended as building blocks. Begin with what can be achieved.

Conclusion

A culture of collaboration enriches every aspect of the educational environment. In such a community, participants generate new ideas and fresh ways of looking at things. The results include students being more involved in their own learning and educators experiencing greater creativity because of the synergy of shared planning. According to *Information Power: Building Partnerships for Learning* (AASL & AECT, 1998) what emerges is a "vibrant and engaged community of learners" (p. 51).

Although they are not easy to achieve, collaborative partnerships are worth striving for in today's schools. The outcomes are more than a sum of the parts. Such partnerships profoundly change our approach to improvement in our classrooms and library media centers. Bush (2003) states it well when she concludes, "What more 'real world' impact can our practice have than to help us teach that change is possible when we listen to and learn about ourselves and others and act together toward a mutually agreed upon goal?" (p. 70).

Figure 3.9: Strategies to Build Collaborative Relationships

Strategies	Possible actions
Be visible and approachable	• Be friendly. • Make time for everyone. • Serve on curriculum committees. • Attend school-wide planning meetings. • Keep busy administrators informed. • Work with your student council. • Participate in parent-teacher meetings.
Communicate	• Use e-mail. • Write thank you notes. • Do short reports of planning sessions and disseminate them to team members. • Contribute to the school newspaper. • Contribute to faculty and family bulletins. • Contact local press and television about major collaborative events.
Start small	• Begin with a willing teacher. • Begin with one interested department or grade level. • Be proactive. • Work with a new teacher. • Orient student teachers assigned to your school. • Volunteer to lead or assist with staff development sessions that deal with technology or literacy. • Be vigilant about ways to support your departments and grade levels.
Think "big picture"	• Volunteer to serve on vision teams. • Suggest ways to map or track the school curriculum. • Serve on policy-making committees. • Attend in-service sessions that target standards-based learning and inquiry-focused teaching.

4 Designing Inquiry-Driven Instruction

What Is Critical in Designing Inquiry-Driven Instruction?

Three fundamental questions must be addressed in planning all meaningful learning experiences:

- What do we want students to learn?
- How will we know if learning has occurred?
- How will we facilitate the learning process?

What do we want students to learn?

This first question challenges us to think critically about learning that really matters. It requires that we prioritize the targets of learning and find a focus for that learning. In inquiry learning, there are at least three major strands and related questions that we must consider, namely:

- Content knowledge—What content will help students understand the concept or problem? Will they be able to transfer this understanding to other situations?
- Skills—What reading, writing, and inquiry skills will students need to understand and to deal with this concept or problem?
- Thinking processes—What thinking skills and dispositions are essential for learning to occur?

In schools where content standards are central to the curriculum, the above questions must be answered in light of the standards. Inquiry learning focuses on how students construct meaning and solve problems. Hence it is crucial to identify those standards that embody the inquiry process. For example, in designing a unit that focuses on an environmental problem or theme, teachers and library media specialists must select standards that deal with the scientific method of investigation as well as standards that address environmental themes in social studies and science.

> **This chapter:**
> - Identifies key elements in designing inquiry-driven instruction.
> - Suggests a design strategy that starts with clear goals and assessment measures.
> - Focuses on specific approaches that use an inquiry-driven framework.
> - Describes the integration of information literacy standards in inquiry learning.

How will we know if learning has occurred?

This question has two important parts to it. First, we must consider how students will demonstrate their learning; and second, we must decide how best to assess the quality of that demonstration.

How can we motivate youngsters to demonstrate their learning in deeper and more creative ways? The traditional paper and pencil test seldom allows students to display either the breadth or the depth of their newly acquired knowledge. Along similar lines, the ten-page report assignment often reflects the students' copying talents more than their thinking processes.

Inquiry learning entails working with students to determine what makes a product purposeful. When student work is not restricted to tests and to traditional reports, students often blossom into motivated learners. There is excitement and energy when the youngsters are able to showcase their learning through products ranging from multimedia slide shows and videotapes to drama productions and creative writing. These products stretch students to take facts and data and to analyze and create personal meaning from them. The products reflect synthesis and application because students must connect pieces of information in ways that make sense to them.

Importantly, there must be real audiences for the products. These audiences may range from peer groups and families to community boards and local businesses. The essential factor is having real people who will hear, view, and read the finished work.

Deciding on a product is only part of the challenge. The other critical part is determining how the quality of a product will be measured. Inquiry learning requires that the product embody the soundness of students' conclusions based on questioning, planning, searching, collecting, and interpreting data. In other words, inquiry learning demands that we evaluate not only the quality of the content but that we assess the process by which that content is acquired. To do this we need to wrestle with questions as follows:

- What criteria will we use to assess the content of the product?
- What criteria will we use to assess the process?
- How will we identify gradations of performance for each criterion?

How will we facilitate the learning process?

This question focuses on the roles of teacher, library media specialist, and other instructors involved in a collaborative team approach to teaching. Inquiry learning encourages instructors to do more guiding and consulting than direct teaching. However, it does not preclude explicit instruction where it might be needed. Questions that help us determine which roles to take include the following:

- What do students already know? How might we build on this foundation?
- What don't they know? What is the most effective method to provide this necessary information?
- Who on the team is best qualified to take the lead at different stages of the project?

The responses to the above questions will differ based on the needs of the students, the nature of the project, and the talents and strengths of the collaborators.

Along with the issue of roles and responsibilities, planners must determine the sequence and nature of specific learning tasks that facilitate the learning process. In inquiry learning, the planners might start with tentative ideas about specific tasks. However, since student involvement is critical in this type of learning, tasks may change as students help to assess their own progress and give voice to their own questions and interests. The collaborating instructors must be ready and willing to adapt their plans as the unit evolves.

Where Do We Start in Designing Inquiry-Driven Instruction?

Let's consider where many teachers and library media specialists start in traditional planning. They often begin with ideas for activities. Hence they integrate content areas by finding a topic that lends itself to a variety of activities. Here is a typical scenario:

> *Kindergarten teachers decided to work on a unit on apples. During math time, students sorted, counted, and measured apples. They converted apples into applesauce as a health and nutrition activity. In science, they saw a short video on how apples were grown. The library media specialists read them stories with apples in the title. During art time, the youngsters drew apples, then cut and pasted them on paper trees. Just for fun, they also bobbed for apples.*

Children certainly enjoyed all of these activities; however, enjoyment alone does not make the unit inquiry-based. As Short and others (1996) have noted, curriculum fashioned around topics in the manner described above is still fragmented. Individual subjects are being taught in isolation. Learning consists of a string of "fun" activities that are incidentally connected to a general topic. There is no "big idea" or "big question" that focuses the learning experience. In the above scenario, students were also not involved in decisions about what to learn, how to learn, or how to judge their own success. Because it was unclear just what students were supposed to learn about apples, it was impossible to assess whether or not learning targets had been met.

In designing inquiry-driven instruction, rather than starting with the activities, planners start with an idea of what they want students to perform at the end of the learning experience. Wiggins and McTighe (1998) have popularized the term "backward design" (p. 146) to describe this essential concept. Other educators including Perkins (1992), Wiske (1994), and Mitchell (1995) have advocated similar approaches to curriculum design.

In these various models, unit designers first articulate what students will be able to demonstrate at the end of a unit and how they plan to assess students' performance. Decisions on specific activities and tasks follow these critical initial steps. Planning in this fashion includes the elements outlined in Figure 4.1.

Figure 4.1: Planning with the Outcome in Mind

1. **Identify learning outcomes and product.**
   - What is the concept or problem?
   - What are students expected to learn?
   - How will they demonstrate what they learned?

2. **Align the outcomes with standards that address both content and process.**
   - Which standards relate to the concept or problem selected?
   - Which standards relate to the inquiry process?

3. **Establish criteria to assess performance.**
   - What criteria are essential to measure a quality product?
   - What criteria are essential to determine mastery of the inquiry process?

4. **Devise methods to measure levels of performance.**
   - What strategies can we use to assess performance (e.g., conferencing, role-playing)?
   - What tools might we create to assess performance (e.g., rubric, checklist)?

5. **Identify the essential questions that frame the unit.**
   - What are the big questions that reflect the concept selected? OR
   - What are the big questions that reflect the problem selected?

6. **Create a tentative outline of activities that foster an inquiry approach to learning.**
   - How do we motivate curiosity and questions about a problem or concept?
   - How do we encourage predictions and hypotheses related to the problem?
   - How do we build skills in locating, retrieving, and organizing data related to the problem?
   - How do we develop abilities to synthesize, analyze, and interpret information?
   - How do we invite creative demonstrations of new knowledge?
   - How do we promote self-reflection?

This design process has important implications for how an instructional team approaches its work and how students learn. It begins with the identification of clearly defined goals. It also requires the generation of compelling questions to drive the learning.

What Approaches Reflect an Inquiry-Driven Framework?

What types of approaches place the how of learning on an equal plane with the what of learning? We suggest two interrelated approaches in this chapter: curriculum built around themes and around problems or issues. Neither approach is new; however, both are potentially powerful means to develop inquiry learning.

Theme-based learning

In practice a thematic unit is usually interdisciplinary and broad in scope. It involves students in learning that is personally meaningful and important to learn about (Unger, 1994). To be effective the unit plan should incorporate three components of curriculum design—content, skills, and assessments (Jacobs, 2000). Students use reading and writing skills as they pose questions and seek understanding of the larger theme or concept. Importantly, the thematic approach provides a context for developing thinking skills and dispositions that are necessary for in-depth learning.

The key to theme-based instruction is identifying topics that generate a variety of possible concepts and approaches (Unger, 1994; Perkins, 1992). For practitioners the question becomes, "How do we distinguish topics from themes?" Figure 4.2 provides several examples of subject-based units that have been expanded into generative themes.

Figure 4.2: Comparing Topics and Themes

Topic		Theme
Butterflies	$\Longrightarrow$	Life cycles
Underground Railroad	$\Longrightarrow$	Racism
Coral reef	$\Longrightarrow$	Interdependence
Chinese New Year	$\Longrightarrow$	Cultural awareness

Themes are central to a discipline and understandable and accessible to students. They must also provide opportunities to make connections across content areas and offer many avenues of exploration (Wiske, 1994). It is critical to use national, state, or district standards in identifying possible themes.

Because the purpose of theme-based instruction is to involve students in an in-depth study that emphasizes process as well as content, the initial planning done by the instructional team provides a framework rather than a rigid, predetermined series of activities. While the instructors must identify targets and means of assessment, students also participate in some of the decisions about what will be learned, how it will be learned, and what criteria will be used to assess the learning.

A summary of strategies to develop a theme-based unit is presented in Figure 4.3.

Figure 4.3: How to Develop a Theme-Based Unit

1. Start by examining the content and performance standards required by your state.
2. Look for a generative topic, a major concept, or a big idea that cuts across content areas. This is your theme.
3. Determine how students will demonstrate knowledge.
    -   Identify the performance task.
    -   Select the criteria to assess the product and process.
4. Transform the theme into framing questions.
5. Create a web or mind map to show different aspects of the theme.
6. Select promising aspects to study in depth. Consider the following:
    -   Interests and needs of students.
    -   Connections to the real world.
7. Devise an instructional plan that includes an inquiry method of learning.
8. Determine which steps in the process will require direct instruction, guided practice, or other instructional interventions.
9. Develop a list of student and teacher resources.

Example of theme-based instruction

Let's take a look at a middle school unit designed around a theme. We use the steps in Figure 4.3 to describe the development process.

1. **Start by examining the content and performances standards required by your state.**
    A core team of middle school teachers along with the library media specialist and the technology coordinator examined and prioritized content standards for the areas of social studies, language arts, and information literacy. They selected the following standards as instructional targets:

    -   World History, Standard 1: Long-term changes and recurring patterns in history (National Center for History in the Schools, n.d.).
    -   National Geography, Standard 17: How to apply geography to interpret the present and plan for the future (National Geographic Society, n.d.).
    -   Language Arts, Standard 1: Students read a wide range of print and nonprint texts to build an understanding of texts, of themselves, and of the cultures of the United States and the world; to acquire new information, to respond to the needs and demands of society and the workplace, and for personal fulfillment (National Council of Teachers of English & International Reading Association, n.d.).
    -   Language Arts, Standard 7: Students conduct research on issues and interests by generating ideas and questions, and by posing problems. They gather, evaluate, and synthesize data from a variety of sources (e.g., print and nonprint texts, artifacts, people) to communicate their discoveries in ways that suit their purpose

and audience (National Council of Teachers of English & International Reading Association, n.d.).

- Information Literacy, Standard 3: The student who is information literate uses information accurately and creatively (AASL & AECT, 1998).
- Information Literacy, Standard 9: The student who contributes positively to the learning community and to society is information literate and participates effectively in groups to pursue and generate information (AASL & AECT, 1998).

2. **Look for a generative topic, a major concept, or a big idea that cuts across content areas. This is your theme.**

The planning team searched for a theme that would resonate with students while addressing the required content standards. They wanted a theme that offered opportunities for students to make connections on a personal level as well as with other topics. They also wanted a theme that was rich in possibilities so that literature, music, and other arts could be infused in a purposeful way. They finally decided upon the theme of conflict.

3. **Determine how students will demonstrate knowledge.**

The planners worked on a performance task that would drive the learning and serve as a basis for determining whether students had met the targeted standards. Together with the students, they designed the following culminating product.

▶ *We will develop a Web site on the theme of conflict that will be accessible to other students and to the community at large. With partners we will create a page on global conflict that:*

- *Provides background about a specific area of global conflict.*
- *Analyzes the causes of the conflict with reference to the history of the region.*
- *Explains the connection between the current conflict and past history.*
- *Includes a map that shows the location of the hot spot.*
- *Explores the consequences of ignoring the conflict.*
- *Suggests possible solutions to the conflict.*
- *Presents a graphic representation of the conflict.*
- *Solicits questions and feedback from Web site visitors.*

The instructors involved students in setting the criteria for assessing their Web pages (Figure 4.4).

In addition to the product, the information search process was assessed through observation, conferencing, self-reflection, and examination of students' questions, notes, and other work products.

Figure 4.4: Assessment Criteria for Student Web Pages

What needs to be assessed?	What are the criteria for successful performance?
Content	• Does the presentation address all of the components described in the performance task? • Is the information accurate? • Is there enough information? • Is the information relevant to the theme of conflict? • Are the sources of information cited?
Writing	• Is the main theme or idea clearly expressed and supported with interesting and relevant details? • Is the organization logical and easy to follow? • Does the author use precise language to convey meaning? • Does the writing adhere to the conventions of spelling, grammar, and usage?
Presentation	• Do the pictures, color, and sound help people to understand the message? • Are the graphic presentations well designed and appropriate for the content? • Do headers, text boxes, and other graphic features help to organize and describe the content? • Are buttons used to help with navigation?

4. **Transform the theme into framing questions.**
   The unit planners decided to begin with a question that would provoke middle school students to think about conflicts in their own lives. They asked, "What are the areas of conflict in your world?" The following questions were added to guide the learning toward the selected content standards for history and geography:

   - What are the causes of conflict?
   - What are the effects of conflict?
   - How can conflict be resolved?
   - What examples of conflict can you find throughout history?

   These questions became the focus for the class inquiry. As students worked in groups to investigate different areas of conflict, they were encouraged to make generalizations based upon their findings.

5. **Create a web or mind map to show different aspects of the theme.**
Although the instructors developed a skeleton web, they wanted students to collaborate on their own webs. The team used a web (Figure 4.5) to generate discussion about areas of conflict that might affect their students' lives. The goal was to motivate students to think about conflict from different perspectives and to reflect this group thinking in their own webs.

Although most of the webs produced by student groups contained elements similar to the teachers' web, the students added many details to clarify what they meant by conflict in their personal lives, in school, in the community, and in the world.

Figure 4.5: Web Showing Possible Areas of Conflict

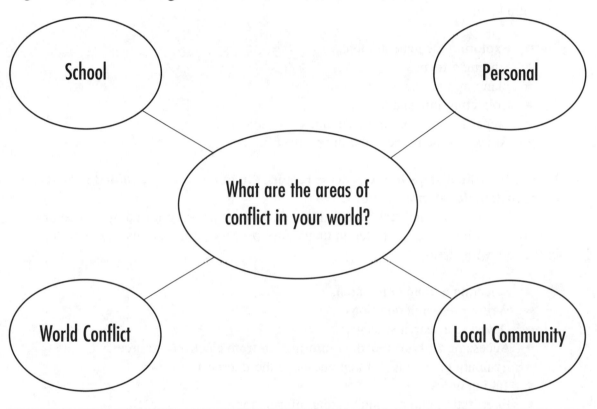

6. **Select promising aspects to study in depth.**
Students immediately seized upon the issue of conflict in school. They cited playground incidents, squabbles with friends, and perceptions about fairness in the classroom.

Because this was a thematic unit, the concept of conflict was addressed in many different ways. Students explored conflict as a theme in literature, and they practiced conflict resolution strategies through dramatization and role-play. These activities were valuable in helping students develop a basic understanding of the nature of conflict.

7. **Devise an instructional plan that includes an inquiry method of learning.**
Students began by reflecting on conflict in their own lives — at home, in the classroom, on the playground, and in the community. Groups of students presented scenarios that required their classmates to identify the source of conflict and brainstorm ways of deal-

ing with it. Conflict resolution techniques were introduced; and students were encouraged to use this process throughout the year whenever conflict arose.

As students became familiar with the theme and its application to their own lives, teachers encouraged them to look beyond their immediate situations for conflict in the larger community and in the world. Homework assignments involved watching television news shows, skimming through newspaper headlines, reading magazines, and following news reports on the World Wide Web.

Class discussions focused on identifying world "hot spots" or potential areas of conflict around the world. Students then formed search teams to investigate major areas of global conflict. The library media specialist worked with subject area teachers to introduce the information search process as a method of learning. The process included the following:

- Exploring the general topic.
- Finding a focus.
- Planning the search.
- Collecting information.
- Preparing and presenting findings.
- Assessing the process and the product.

8. **Determine which steps in the process require direct instruction, guided practice, or other instructional interventions.**

The instructional team decided that direct instruction followed by guided practice would be needed at each step in the inquiry process. Mini-lessons were developed in the following areas:

- Selecting a topic to research.
- Writing research questions.
- Devising a search strategy.
- Accessing and downloading information from electronic sources.
- Evaluating content (with emphasis on the Internet).
- Taking notes.
- Interpreting and communicating information.
- Citing sources.

Instruction always focused on a particular skill or process and was followed immediately by ample time for guided practice. Generally speaking, the teachers took responsibility for providing direct instruction when the classroom was the center for the learning, and the library media specialist usually took the lead in the library. Both the teachers and the library media specialist provided feedback and guidance as students worked on the tasks of accessing, analyzing, and synthesizing information. The technology coordinator worked directly with students as they designed their Web pages.

9. **Develop a list of student and teacher resources.**
Because initial discussion on the unit began months before its implementation, the library media specialist was able to purchase the resources needed to support the inquiry process.

She subscribed to local newspapers for each class and added major news magazines to the periodical collection. She also provided access to an online magazine database.

In addition, the library media specialist examined the central collection for resources dealing with potential areas of global conflict. Based on this analysis, she purchased print and nonprint materials that met the criteria of accuracy, authority, timeliness, and age appropriateness. She also searched for materials that represented diverse points of view on an issue.

Problem-based learning

Like theme-based instruction, problem-based learning is an approach that incorporates an inquiry process. Problem-based learning is defined as a statement of a real-life scenario designed to challenge learners, promote the acquisition of knowledge, encourage the development of effective problem-solving and critical thinking skills, and require collaboration with peers. Typically, scenarios focus on current events, the students' life, field of study, or line of work. Importantly the most effective problems are complex, open-ended, and do not have one right solution. (Harper-Marinick, 2001)

While the use of problem-based learning originated in medical schools over thirty years ago, variant forms of it have since been used in education. Harper-Marinick (2001) succinctly describes the process as follows:

Students are encouraged to work in small groups as they determine what information they already have and what information they still need to solve the problem. Brainstorming possible solutions is an essential part of the inquiry process. Analyzing causes and effects are also crucial. Before collecting information, groups develop plans of action that describe what they are investigating and how they plan to undertake this work. A good deal of the student interaction focuses on comparisons and reviews during the data collection and interpretation phases. Team members continually assess their progress in light of what they are discovering. The instructors become facilitators, who ask challenging questions, make resources available, and monitor the problem-solving process.

Strategies to develop a problem-based unit are outlined in Figure 4.6.

Figure 4.6: How to Develop a Problem-Based Unit

1. Select an issue or problem that reflects complex issues and real-world application. It should extend across curriculum lines and appeal to students.
2. Identify content standards embraced by this problem or issue.
3. Determine the essential questions and identify different aspects of the problem.
4. Determine how students will demonstrate what they learn.
5. Identify criteria to assess student performance.
6. Integrate the inquiry process into the investigation.
7. Organize students into groups to conduct in-depth investigations.
8. Facilitate the information search process.
9. Build ongoing assessment by instructors and students into the process.
10. Evaluate student findings and plan for areas of further inquiry.

Example of problem-based instruction

Here is an example of a high school unit focusing on a problem. We use the steps in Figure 4.6 to describe the design process.

1. **Select an issue or problem that reflects complex issues and real-world application. It should extend across curriculum lines and appeal to the students.**

   With the help of the library media specialist, the science teacher invited a marine biologist to speak to her tenth grade science class. He brought along slides to show how Hawaii's shorelines have been receding at an average of 1.25 feet a year. This meant that the state had lost as much as 30% of its shoreline over the last hundred years. The students, who spend their weekends swimming and surfing off the Oahu shoreline, were appalled by these statistics and wanted to alert the public about the situation. They decided to tackle the issue of beach erosion and what people might do to preserve the land.

2. **Identify content standards embraced by this problem or issue.**

   Working together, the library media specialist and teacher identified key state and national standards in three areas:

   - Science: Explains the effect of large and small disturbances on systems in the natural world. Identifies and explains current issues based on evidence found in available information. Collects, organizes, and analyzes information from reliable sources to identify alternative solutions (Hawaii Department of Education, 2002).
   - Language arts: Generates questions, identifies issues, and investigates answers using a range of sources. Evaluates and synthesizes information from research and integrates information with own ideas (Hawaii Department of Education, 2002).
   - Information literacy: Accesses information efficiently and effectively. Evaluates information critically. Uses information accurately. Strives for excellence in information seeking and knowledge generation. Participates effectively in groups to pursue and generate knowledge (AASL & AECT, 1998).

3. **Determine the essential questions and identify different aspects of the problem.**

   Working together, the teacher and students created a mind map (Figure 4.7) that focused on the framing question for their investigation. They also brainstormed various facets of the problem that might be investigated.

   Students formed discussion groups to decide which subtopics were essential in understanding and dealing with the problem. They considered the following:

   - What kind of information would this subtopic provide?
   - How would this information help us understand the problem?
   - How would this information help us resolve the problem?
   - Is there something missing from our mind map?

Figure 4.7: Mind Map for Problem of Beach Erosion

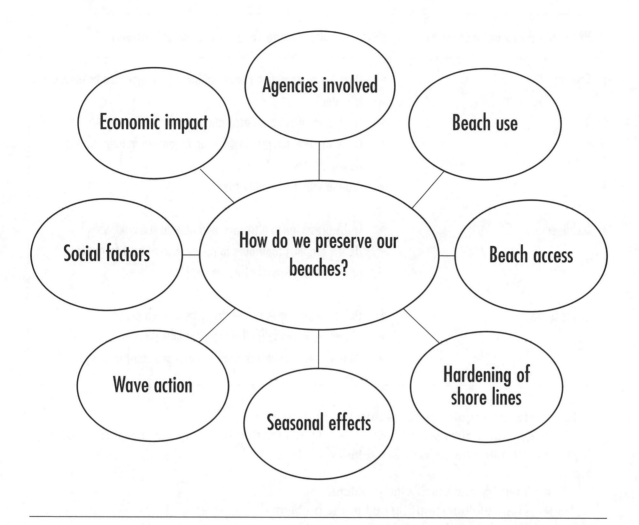

4. **Determine how students will demonstrate what they learn.**
   Students brainstormed possible ways they might communicate their results to a larger public. They decided to create multimedia slide presentations and share them at community board meetings in their neighborhoods.

5. **Identify criteria to assess student performance.**
   The instructional team drafted criteria to assess the slide presentations and sought input from the students. Figure 4.8 reflects their combined effort.
   A ratings checklist was created based on the criteria in Figure 4.8. Students used it to critique their own work and to comment on peer products. The instructors also used the checklist to assess as well as evaluate the presentations. In addition, students maintained investigation journals in which they reflected on their information gathering progress.

Figure 4.8: Assessment Criteria for Multimedia Slide Presentations

What needs to be assessed?	What are the criteria for successful performance?
Content	• Does the presentation clearly address the major idea or message intended? • Is supporting evidence accurate and relevant? • Is the information presented in an organized manner that is clearly understood? • Are the sources properly cited?
Multimedia	• Is the presentation attractive and easy to read and view? • Do the graphics contribute to rather than detract from the presentation's overall effectiveness?
Collaboration	• Did the team capitalize on strengths of each member? • Did all members fulfill their responsibilities? • Were disagreements resolved or managed constructively?

6. **Integrate the inquiry process into the investigation.**
   The teacher and library media specialist developed the following outline of the inquiry process to frame the activities and tasks for the unit:

   - Identify and clarify the problem.
   - Generate questions related to the problem.
   - Determine what information is needed.
   - Strategize how to get needed information.
   - Collect information and discuss initial evidence.
   - Monitor progress.
   - Organize and plan for use of information.
   - Prepare and present findings.
   - Reflect on efforts.

7. **Organize students into groups to conduct in-depth investigations.**
   Students worked in pairs or small groups on different aspects of the problem. They used the subtopics they had mapped to select their focuses.

8. **Facilitate the information search process.**
   The inquiry process naturally flowed into a search for information. The library media specialist taught students how to access and evaluate online resources and primary documents. She also helped students to contact local resource people and suggested ways to conduct effective interviews by phone and e-mail. In addition, she assisted students in

taking better notes and facilitated discussions on the accuracy and authority of the information that students were collecting.

9. **Build ongoing assessment by instructors and students into the process.**
Whether the sessions were conducted in the classroom or in the library media center, students were required to spend a few minutes at the end of each period writing their thoughts in their investigation journals. Prompts they used included:

- How well are we doing?
- What have we learned about the problem studied?
- What difficulties are we encountering?
- What alternative strategies should we try?

The library media specialist and teacher kept their own informal observation notes based on student interaction and dialogue. Using the student journals and their own notes, they modified the learning experience as they progressed.

10. **Evaluate student presentations and plan for areas of further inquiry.**
Students participated in the creation of a rating checklist to evaluate their presentations. They also discussed their progress and final accomplishments using the following guide questions:

- How well did we do? How do we know this?
- What did we learn about the problem studied?
- What did we learn about ourselves?
- What would we do differently next time? Why?
- What additional questions do we have?
- How might we pursue these questions?

Similarities between theme-based and problem-based learning

Both thematic and problem-based curricula embody the essential characteristics of inquiry-driven learning. Figure 4.9 illustrates their similarities.

How Might Information Literacy Standards Be Integrated Into These Approaches?

The information literacy process is woven into the fabric of inquiry-based learning. Pappas (1998) indicates the relationship between information literacy and this type of learning is a symbiotic one. The learner must gather, evaluate, and use information critically, efficiently, and creatively. Library media specialists, who are looking for ways to collaborate on curriculum, find that the methods and tools of inquiry provide a fertile field for sowing the seeds of information literacy (Pappas & Tepe, 2002).

Figure 4.9: Similarities Between Theme-Based and Problem-Based Learning

Key Questions	Similarities
Who decides what is learned?	• Curriculum is negotiated between teachers and students.
What do students learn?	• Students learn concepts that provide a framework for connecting isolated pieces of information. • They examine problems and issues that relate to their world. • They demonstrate their communication skills. • They effectively access, organize, and present information. • They think critically and solve problems.
Where does the learning occur?	• Learning occurs in the classroom, library media center, technology and science labs, and community.
How do students learn?	• Curriculum is organized around broad, open-ended topics or problems. • Students pose questions that guide the inquiry. • They investigate through hands-on experiments and research. • They collaborate on analysis and problem solving. • They prepare and present their findings. • They practice continual reflection.
Why use these approaches?	• Student learning extends beyond acquisition of facts. • Students learn to use disciplinary tools and methods (e.g., those of scientist, historian). • Students create knowledge. • Students have a stake in what is studied. • Students are more apt to retain and to apply what they have learned.

As examples, we identify the Information Literacy Standards (AASL & AECT, 1998) embedded in the two units described in this chapter (Figures 4.10 and 4.11).

The information literacy standards included in Figures 4.10 and 4.11 come from *Information Power: Building Partnerships for Learning* by American Association of School Librarians and Association for Educational Communications and Technology. © 1998. American Library Association and Association for Educational Communications and Technology. Reprinted by permission of the American Library Association.

Figure 4.10: Middle School Unit on Conflict

Information literacy standard	Evidence of standard in practice
Standard 1: Accesses information efficiently and effectively.	• Used various resources to collect information relevant to the inquiry. • Downloaded information from electronic resources and took notes from print materials.
Standard 2: Evaluates information critically and competently.	• Evaluated information for relevance, accuracy, and completeness. • Identified bias in articles.
Standard 3: Uses information accurately and creatively.	• Synthesized information from various resources. • Incorporated principles of design in the Web pages and created a graphic representation to symbolize the conflict.
Standard 4: Pursues information related to students' interests.	• Selected topics of personal interest to research.
Standard 6: Strives for excellence in information seeking and knowledge generation.	• Set criteria for topics, questions, notes, and presentations. • Used checklists and rubrics to assess work throughout the project.
Standard 7: Recognizes the importance of information to a democratic society.	• Focused on root causes of a global problem and examined data to look at problems from multiple points of view. • Shared information and exchanged viewpoints through Web pages.
Standard 8: Practices ethical behavior in regard to information and information technology.	• Cited sources and created bibliographies. • Adhered to school policies regarding the ethical use of technology.
Standard 9: Participates effectively in groups to pursue and generate information.	• Developed assessment criteria and used rubrics as a basis for peer performance assessment.

Figure 4.11: High School Unit on Beach Erosion

Information literacy standard	Evidence of standard in practice
Standard 1: Accesses information efficiently and effectively.	• Conducted print and online searches and retrieved information from both primary and secondary resources. • Conducted interviews by phone and e-mail.
Standard 2: Evaluates information critically and competently.	• Conferred with peers and with instructors to determine the accuracy, currency, and authority of their information.
Standard 3: Uses information accurately and creatively.	• Created multimedia slide presentations that demonstrated students' ability to analyze, synthesize, and present reasoned solutions to the problem studied.
Standard 6: Strives for excellence in information seeking and knowledge generation.	• Continually assessed their own progress through their journals and discussions with peers and instructors.
Standard 7: Recognizes the importance of information to a democratic society.	• Communicated findings at community board meetings. • Expressed a need for assuming responsible stewardship for the state's beaches.
Standard 8: Practices ethical behavior in regard to information and information technology.	• Checked for accuracy of all statements. • Properly acknowledged all sources used.
Standard 9: Participates effectively in groups to pursue and generate information.	• Worked in teams and small groups. • Continually assessed communication and problem solving skills as a team.

Conclusion

Inquiry-driven instruction extends beyond the *what, when*, and *where* of events, places, and peoples. It engages both instructors and students in investigations that demand careful examination of the *how*, *why*, and *what if* of situations. Instructors face the challenge of shifting from topical teaching to an emphasis on concepts and issues that generate more complex levels of thinking and that require an appreciation of multiple perspectives. With students as partners, they search for ways to connect learning to personal levels of meaning and to thoughtful levels of action that impact people's lives in a global community.

5 Assessing Learning and Teaching

Why Is Assessment Vital?

In chapter 4 we discussed the importance of planning with the outcome in mind. A critical component of such planning is assessment. This is not an "end of lesson or end of unit phenomenon; [assessment] has to be incorporated at the beginning, at the end, and everywhere in between" (Brimijoin, Marquissee & Tomlinson, 2003, p. 72).

A systematic approach to assessment includes classroom assessment as well as standardized testing. According to Stiggins (1997), the primary purpose of all assessment is "to inform decisions" (p. 24). The need for assessment data as a basis for sound decision-making is evident at every level of the educational hierarchy:

- Students assess to guide independent learning and to monitor and celebrate their own progress.
- Teachers assess to make decisions about how to modify instruction to improve learning.
- Parents use assessment data to keep track of their children's progress.
- School administrators need assessment results to make decisions concerning program support, budget allocations, and professional development activities.
- Policy makers, including the district office, the school board, lawmakers, and community groups, rely on assessment data to set directions and to determine system-wide policies.

Although all of these uses of assessment data are critical, we are most concerned with the classroom and library media center applications of assessment that directly affect teaching and learning. Our targets are:

- Improved student learning.
- Improved strategies for teaching.
- Recognition of students' progress in relation to standards.

> ## This chapter:
> - Addresses why assessment is vital.
> - Explains how assessment differs from evaluation.
> - Discusses what should be assessed.
> - Suggests strategies and tools to assess learning.
> - Discusses who should do the assessing.

Inquiry-based learning requires that students demonstrate their understanding through explanation, interpretation, and application. The information search process, which is embedded in inquiry, is also multi-dimensional in that it requires students to think about a problem or an issue in many different ways. In addition, the search process culminates in products and performances that reflect a unique perspective on a problem or an issue. All of these facets of learning need to be assessed to see if goals are being met.

How Does Assessment Differ from Evaluation?

Although assessment and evaluation are often treated as synonymous terms, there are substantive differences between the two concepts. Donham (1998) views assessment as a collegial process, which involves careful judgment based upon observation. Evaluation, on the other hand, lacks the element of collegiality. It involves placing a value on something.

Evaluation happens at the end of a learning cycle. Data are collected and judgments are formed based upon the evidence. The results of the evaluation are used to modify the program or to make decisions that affect future directions or resource allocations. Evaluation results are often reported as grades. In this case, the evaluation is a judgment about the value of the student's work.

Assessment, on the other hand, is an ongoing activity. It happens throughout the learning process so that the results can be used to modify instruction and to improve student performance. It is important to note "assessment is usually done *with* the student, while evaluation is done *to* the student's work" (AASL & AECT, 1998, p. 173). While evaluation and assessment are both critical, in this chapter we focus on the role of assessment in the instructional process.

What Should Be Assessed?

The word "targets" has been used as an umbrella term for the goals, expectations, and desired outcomes of learning (Stiggins, 1997; Wiggins & McTighe, 1998). Instructional design starts with a precise statement of these targets. Students, as well as teachers, need to know in advance what they are expected to know and be able to do. They also need to know the standards that will be used to judge their products and performances (Wiggins & McTighe, 1998). Along with process skills that are important in information searching and use, instructional targets must also include thinking skills and dispositions and the products and performances that represent students' understanding of the content.

We might start by asking ourselves questions that help us identify the targets of learning involved in inquiry and information searching. Figure 5.1 displays how a high school social studies teacher worked with the library media specialist to identify the instructional targets for a thematic unit examining how the Civil War changed the fabric of American society. The driving questions for the unit were

- What differences separated the North from the South before the Civil War?
- How did these differences contribute to the conflict?
- What were the lasting effects of the war on American society?

Figure 5.1: Identifying Instructional Targets for a Civil War Unit

Targets	Questions	Instructional goals
Content knowledge	What are the important concepts to be learned?	Students will: • Compare social, political, and economic differences between the North and South. • Examine role of slavery in the conflict. • Analyze how the war and reconstruction changed the course of U.S. history.
Process skills	What skills will students need to investigate the topic?	Students will: • Use the research process to locate, analyze, and interpret information. • Use a variety of sources. • Use evidence to support a personal point of view related to the war and its influence on American society.
Thinking skills	What problem solving strategies will students need to use? What critical thinking skills will be required?	Students will: • Identify the problem or issue. • Analyze causes and effects. • Suggest possible solutions. • Take a personal stand. • Support stand with evidence.
Products and performances	What products and/or performances can students create to demonstrate their knowledge and skill?	In their products, students will: • Express a point of view. • Answer their research questions accurately. • Use data to justify a position. • Observe conventions appropriate to the presentation.
Values, attitudes, or habits of mind	What do we want students to care about?	Students will be actively engaged in open and honest communication about the issues involved.

How Should the Learning Be Assessed?

Educators often discover that there is a startling gap between what they teach and what students actually learn. Current research indicates that educators need to identify more effective and precise ways to measure how students are progressing in relation to goals and expectations. As schools move from a linear, textbook-based learning environment towards a more authentic curriculum, the emphasis has shifted to performance-based assessments that require the application of knowledge and skills in new situations.

The need for more authentic forms of assessment has been well documented (Perkins, 1992; Stiggins, 1997; Wiggins & McTighe, 1998). Callison (1998) explains authentic assessment as a process that involves "multiple forms of performance measurement reflecting students' learning, achievement, motivation, and attitudes on instructionally relevant activities" (p. 42).

This is not to say that pencil and paper tests are not valid instruments for assessing students' knowledge. If, for example, we want to know whether students understand the causes of the Civil War, a multiple choice or fill-in-the-blanks quiz might be one measure. The challenge is to clearly understand our targets and to find the most appropriate means of assessing them.

Stiggins (1997) maintains that quality assessment lies in the ability of educators to match assessment purposes and targets with the appropriate tools and strategies. Several assessment strategies that work well in inquiry-based experiences include the following (e.g., Donham, 1998; Kearney, 2000; AASL & AECT, 1998):

- Informal checking.
- Checklists.
- Conferencing.
- Graphic organizers.
- Journal writing.
- Rubrics.
- Process-folios.

In the following pages, we describe each of these assessment strategies and provide examples of how they might be used.

Informal checking

Stiggins (1997) indicates that "personal communication" is "one of the most common ways teachers gather information about student achievement" (p. 78) on a daily basis. It involves asking students a question for the purpose of finding out whether they truly understand what they are doing, why they are doing it, or how well they understand the concepts. Although this is an informal method of gathering data, it has a built-in flexibility that allows for follow-up questioning and deeper probing.

Example of informal checking

A kindergarten class is learning about life cycles. They observe the metamorphosis of a monarch butterfly from egg, to larva, to caterpillar, to pupa, to adult butterfly. In the media center they look at books and visit a Web site that illustrates the same process using time-lapse photography. Finally, they draw pictures to show their understanding of the butterfly's life cycle. Throughout the process the teacher and library media specialist check for understanding by asking questions like:

> *What do you see on the leaves? How did it get there?*
> *What is happening inside the chrysalis? How do you know?*
> *What will the adult butterfly do now?*
> *How is the life cycle of the butterfly like the life cycle of the chick?*

Checklists

A checklist is a list of the steps to be taken and the criteria for completion. By serving as a guide for students working through their projects, the checklist is an important tool for student self-assessment. Teachers and library media specialists may use the same instrument to monitor the progress of students as they work through the information search process.

Example of checklist

A second grade class is studying the concept of adaptation by examining life in the sea. Each child selects a marine animal to research. Working with fifth grade research buddies, the younger students follow the research process to learn about their animals. A class matrix is used to summarize the information so that children can draw comparisons, make generalizations, and eventually answer the essential question about how adaptation helps animals to survive. Each child ultimately creates a product in which he describes the animal and gives information related to its feeding habits, its behavior, and other factors related to adaptation. To allow for different learning styles, students "show what they know" in writing and another creative form that might include artwork, a dramatic performance, or a multimedia production.

Second graders use a checklist (Figure 5.2) to assess their progress at each phase of the project. Fifth grade buddies, the teacher, and library media specialist also assess each student's progress using the same tool. Throughout the project, the checklists are used to monitor what is going well and where improvement is needed. The goal is to produce more independent researchers.

Grade Two—Life in the Sea
Assessment of the Research Process

I am studying _____

Put a sticker in the box that tells how well you did each task.

This is what I did	I did it by myself	I did it with help	I cannot do it yet	Comments
I chose a sea animal that is interesting to me.				
I made a web to show what I wanted to find out.				
I found information in at least three different resources.				
I took notes that answered my questions.				
I used my notes to write sentences about my animal.				
I prepared an interesting presentation that showed how my sea animal adapts to life in the sea.				
I presented my knowledge in at least two different ways.				

Conferencing

Conferencing refers to more formal interactions between teachers and students. When the purpose of these interactions is to gather information relevant to the student's learning, the conference becomes an assessment strategy. These more structured interactions are especially useful when students are working on their products or presentations (Harada & Yoshina, 1997). Typically, students sign up for a conference when they think they have enough information to answer their research questions. Although most of the conferences occur between the teacher and student in the classroom, students may also confer with the library media specialist when they need to verify information or to consult additional resources.

Example of conferencing

Ninth grade students are planning their presentations for a school curriculum fair. They schedule a conference with their teacher or library media specialist, who asks some of the following initial questions:

What do you want to accomplish?
What form will your presentation take?
Who will be your audience?
What resources will you need?
Do you have all the information you need?
Do you have enough time to do this presentation?
Who will do what?
What additional help will you need?

Graphic Organizers

Graphic organizers blend assessment with instruction. By breaking down the learning task, a graphic organizer provides a visual representation of the dimensions of a problem, a concept, or a task. Pappas (1997) elaborates:

> They provide learners with a visual structure that allows them to make connections between topics or concepts, relate to prior knowledge, plan a search strategy, select and evaluate information, interpret information, and evaluate the research outcome. (p. 30)

Organizers may range from flow charts and Venn diagrams to T-charts and time lines. We present two commonly used organizers, the K-W-L chart and the web, as examples below.

Example of K-W-L chart

K-W-L charts are used to record:

- What the student *knows* about the topic.
- What the student *wants* to find out about the topic.
- What the student *learned* about the topic.

Prior to learning about the topic, students write everything they know about it in the first column. They then list in the second column questions about the topic that relate to the essential questions for the unit. As they progress with the research, they write what they have learned in the third column. The chart may be used as a starting point for students to reflect upon their learning. It also documents progress by providing a "before" and "after" snapshot of the student's knowledge.

In Figure 5.3 we show how the K-W-L chart was used in conjunction with a sixth grade unit on diversity. This student focused her research on the experience of Japanese immigrants to Hawaii. At the beginning, she listed what she knew about the topic and what she wanted to find out. As she uncovered new information, she also recorded it on the chart.

Example of web

The web is a diagram that provides an overview of a concept or big idea. Webbing, or mind mapping, helps students visually show the connections between related ideas. In the research process webbing might be used to:

- Analyze the different components of the topic, issue, or problem.
- Generate questions about the topic.
- Show relationships among different aspects of a large topic.
- Link notes to questions or subtopics.

A student's web is a graphic representation of his thinking. This makes it a valuable tool for assessing the thinking processes involved in inquiry and information processing. Figure 5.4 is a web created by a ninth grade student who was trying to find a focus for his environmental research. A careful examination of this web reveals several things about how the student processed information. He was able to think divergently about the topic and to look at the concept from different perspectives. Moreover, by linking ideas, he demonstrated an ability to make connections between concepts. Taken in its entirety, the web showed that the student had a notion of "the big picture." Having made this assessment, the teacher could use the web to help the student determine a research focus.

Figure 5.3: K-W-L Chart for Study of Japanese Immigrants to Hawaii

This is what I know	This is what I want to find out	This is what I learned
Many Japanese people came to Hawaii.	Why did they come to Hawaii?	Many Japanese came to Hawaii to earn a better living by working on sugar plantations.
Japanese people were put in camps during WW II.	Why were Japanese people put into camps?	Japanese were sent to camps because the U.S. thought they would be on Japan's side in the war.
Japanese people work in all kinds of jobs.	What kinds of work do Japanese people do?	The first immigrants worked on the sugar cane plantations. Today, Japanese work as doctors, lawyers, teachers, politicians, and any other job they want.
Japanese people like to eat rice and fish but they eat other things, too.	What foods did the Japanese bring to Hawaii?	They brought sushi and musubi (rice balls). On Girls' Day they ate mochi (sweet, steamed rice cakes).
Japanese people like sumo wrestling.	What other customs did the Japanese bring to Hawaii?	New Year's is an important day. They make a lot of different foods, clean their homes, and set off fireworks. They celebrate Boys' Day and Girls' Day in Hawaii. On Boys' Day, people fly cloth carps on poles outside their home. Carps symbolize strength for boys. On Girls' Day, they display doll collections to celebrate the girls in the family.

Figure 5.4: Concept Web for Environmental Research

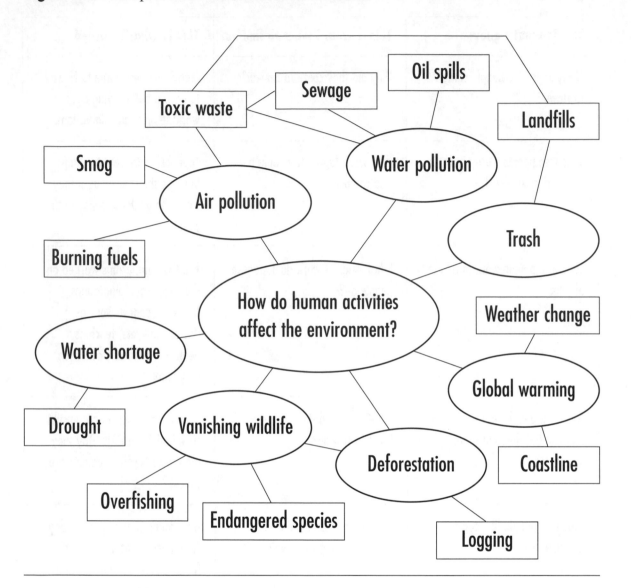

Journal Writing

Journal writing provides one of the most useful tools for assessing growth. Carefully worded prompts can be used to gain insight into how students are dealing with key components of the process, including the acquisition of knowledge. Used judiciously, reflection can provide teachers with information about individual students that would be difficult to gather through any other means. Journal writing allows them to zero in on the thought processes of all students in a group (Harada, 2002).

As students reflect on what they are learning, how they are learning, and how they feel about the process, teachers and library media specialists are in a better position to make adjustments in a timely manner. For students, journal writing provokes them to pause and to reflect on what they are doing and to consider how things are working for them.

Example of journal prompts

To effectively use journal writing as an assessment strategy, instructors provide prompts that are specific to the kinds of information needed. Figure 5.5 suggests prompts that might be used to assess different aspects of the search process.

Figure 5.5: Alignment of Journal Prompts with the Search Process

Steps in the search process	Journal prompts
Explore the general topic.	• What did I learn about the theme or issue? • How does this connect with what I already know? • What resources did I explore?
Find a focus.	• What aspects of the theme or issue did I find interesting and important to learn about? • What questions do I have about this issue or theme?
Plan the research and presentation.	• How will I present my information? Why is this a good plan? • What keywords will I use to search for information? • What are the best resources to consult?
Evaluate and collect information.	• How did I select information to download from the Web? • Which resources were the best? Why? • How did I locate the specific information I needed?
Organize and present information.	• What do I want to say or do in my presentation? • Why is it important to consider my audience? • What part of my presentation plan have I completed? • Where am I having problems? • What do I need to do next?
Assess the product and the process.	• Can I summarize the steps that I followed in researching my theme or issue? • Which steps were most difficult for me? Why? • What criteria did I use to make sure I had a quality presentation? • How do I feel about myself as a researcher? • If I had it to do over, what would I do differently?

Even the youngest children benefit from keeping journals. Second graders used the following My Search Log (Figure 5.6) to describe their content knowledge, thinking dispositions, and attitudes as they worked on a project to create a clean and safe school.

Figure 5.6: Research Log Used in Primary Grades

My name is _____

I am studying _____

Today's date is _____

MY RESEARCH LOG

Today I worked on _____
(step in the process)

I learned that _____
(content knowledge)

One question I have is _____
(continuous questioning)

One problem that I have is _____
(self-assessment — knowledge and skill)

Something I don't understand is _____
(self-assessment — thinking)

_____

This is how I feel today _____
(affective assessment)

Rubrics

A rubric provides a description of successful performance and gives students feedback about their work (AASL & AECT, 1998; Andrade, 2000). A rubric delineates levels of performance for each of the identified criteria; and also presents a developmental approach to assessment that can be used to measure growth as students move from one research project to another. When rubrics are used in conjunction with instruction, they provide students with a blueprint to assess the quality of their own work. Used in this way, rubrics are a powerful tool for learning.

All rubrics have two things in common—a list of criteria for a successful performance and a description of varying levels of performance (Davies, 2000; Andrade, 2000). The key to an effective rubric is a precise description of the performance required for each level of proficiency (Callison, 1998).

Example of rubrics

Here is an extended scenario of how a fifth grade class studying the Westward Movement incorporated the use of rubrics in their investigation. The essential question was: Why was the Westward Movement important in U.S. history?

Supporting questions included

- What events led to the development of the West?
- Who were the people that built the West?
- What obstacles did they face?

Working in teams of two to four, students selected a research focus that centered on either an event or a group of people pivotal to the development of the West. One of their final products was to design a board game challenging players to survive a journey along one of the major trails used by the pioneers.

The teacher and library media specialist identified two types of rubrics for this particular unit. One dealt with a critical component of the research process, note taking. The other focused on a student product, the board game. Students described the levels of performance for the various criteria in both rubrics.

Rubric for note taking

In designing the note-taking rubric, students grappled with the question, "What are the characteristics of good notes?" The discussion of quality led naturally to an activity where the class examined models of student notes to determine which samples reflected acceptable standards, which exceeded the standards, and which did not meet the standards. The teacher and library media specialist used this input from students to draft a rubric that described different levels of quality. The draft was returned to students for their feedback, and revisions were made. Figure 5.7 is the final version of this student-negotiated rubric for note taking.

Figure 5.7: Rubric for Note Taking

Criteria	Doing well	Getting there	Need help
Accuracy	All of my information is accurate.	Most of my information is accurate.	A lot of my information is not accurate.
Completeness	I answer my questions in full detail, including examples, quotes, explanations. I even pose additional questions.	I make general statements and add some details.	I don't have details. Many of my notes don't answer my questions.
Use of own words	All of my notes are in my own words.	Most of my notes are in my own words.	My notes are copied from the resources I used.
Citations	I cite all sources I used.	I cite some sources I used.	I forgot to cite my sources.

The note-taking rubric was a valuable tool for ongoing assessment. It was reviewed on a regular basis as students collected, analyzed, and recorded information. Students were asked to reflect in their journals about whether the rubrics helped them with the note taking process. This is how one student summed up her thoughts:

> I always thought that if you found something about your topic in the book or on the computer, you just copied it onto the paper. Sometimes I would change the words around so that it wouldn't be considered cheating. Now I know that there are good notes, not-so-good notes, and bad notes. I also learned that the notes depend on what the questions are. No matter what, the notes have to give correct information. You can't make it up. And you have to have a lot of details like examples and quotes to back up your ideas. I think rubrics are a good way of reminding yourself of what you have to do while you are doing it.

Rubric for board game

Since the class had no previous experience with creating board games, the instructors decided to develop a rubric that would guide students as they worked on their products. The teacher introduced the activity by having students play with selected board games ("Settlers of Catan," "Lord of the Rings," "Cosmic Encounter"). They then engaged students in a discussion of "What makes a good board game?" Predictably, students said that good games were interesting, exciting, and challenging. Through strategic questioning, the teacher helped students identify additional factors they might consider in designing their own games. Eventually, the class agreed upon the following elements:

- Theme—All games have a theme. In this case the theme would be "The Westward Movement."
- Setting—Whether it is Middle Earth, outer space, or a local village, all games have a setting that is depicted on the board itself. In this game, the setting would be the United States between 1830 and 1880.
- Players—Competition requires players. Sometimes the players try to destroy each other. The players in this game would be anyone who settled the West (e.g., pioneers, explorers, cattlemen, forty-niners, railroad workers).
- Goals—Every game has a goal. In this game, the goal would be a particular destination that is related to the player's reason for going to the West. For example, the goal of a forty-niner would be to reach California so that he could search for gold.
- Obstacles—Games provide obstacles standing in the way of reaching the goal. The weather, the terrain, the wildlife, native people, disease, and other hazards would challenge the players in this game.
- A route—Most games require the players to follow a route to reach their destination. The routes followed in this game would be the major trails to the West.

In the course of the discussion, students also referred to things like creativity and originality as factors that contributed to the entertainment value of a game. The instructional team integrated this input into a rubric that served as an instructional guide and as a tool for assessing the final products. Peer assessment was also encouraged.

During the curriculum fair the students who played each game were asked to assess it using the same rubric that was used by the developers. Figure 5.8 is the final version of the rubric for assessing board games.

Although the creation of the rubric was a time-consuming process, the teacher and library media specialist felt that the benefits made it well worth the expenditure of time. In her reflection log, the teacher noted:

> I admit that I was quite reluctant to embrace the whole idea of rubrics. It seemed to be much too labor-intensive and time-consuming. However, I have changed my mind. My students really got into the discussion of quality. That, in itself, was a worthwhile activity. The real value of the rubric is that it gives students a basis for self-assessing as they work on their projects. This way they know up front how their work will be judged. The rubric has turned out to be a very useful tool for both assessment and instruction.

Figure 5.8: Rubric for Assessing Board Games

Criteria	Exceeding	Satisfying	Emerging
Knowledge of content	Major landforms and waterways are labeled. All information about people and events is historically accurate. Details include landmarks accurate to the time period.	Landforms and waterways are shown but not labeled. Information about people and events is accurate. Some details about the time period are provided.	Map does not show landforms and waterways. Gives little or no historical information. No details about the time period are provided.
Game strategy	Goal and rules are clearly explained. More than four obstacles add interest and excitement. Alternate routes force choices to be made.	Goal is clearly explained. Rules are not always clear. Three or four obstacles are presented. Alternate routes are not used.	Goal and rules are not given. No obstacles are presented. Trails to the West are not shown.
Appearance of board	Drawings are creative and accurate. Overall design is attractive. Background is an accurate and detailed representation of U.S. geography.	Drawings are accurate, but not always creative. Background accurately represents U.S. geography.	Drawings are not accurate or appropriate. Background map is inaccurate.
Entertainment value	Game builds suspense. It provides for lots of interaction. It is challenging.	Game provides for some interaction. It is fun to play.	It is hard to know how to play the game. It is not interesting.

Process-folios

The portfolio is essentially a container that includes documentation of student growth over a period of time. The students' learning targets define what students elect to include in their portfolios. There are different uses for portfolios. A popular type of portfolio is one that displays students' best works. In this type of portfolio, students select samples of what they consider to be their best products. In this section, however, we describe another type of portfolio, the process-folio.

Process-folios differ from best works portfolios in that they provide a record of students' learning as they progress through the different stages in a process. In addition to final projects, process-folios may contain graphic organizers, notes, reflections, and drafts of work in progress as well as any tools students have used to assess learning along the way. Because the process-folio documents how students learn, they help the instructional team diagnose gaps in the learning process and plan for necessary intervention. More importantly, maintaining process-folios fosters student reflection on what they are doing and how successfully they are achieving their targets.

Process-folios can also be a useful tool in communicating with parents. Students can use the process-folios to explain to their parents what they have done during each phase of a project. Often parents are amazed at the sophistication and complexity of the thinking required to produce the end results.

Example of process-folio

Students in a third grade class form teams to decide what will be the best pet to adopt for their classroom. Each student creates a process-folio that includes the following items:

- Journal logs at key points in the information search process.
- Web of animals considered for pets.
- Checklist of tasks completed in the information search process.
- Checklist to assess contributions as a group member.
- Rubric to evaluate notes taken.
- Rubric to evaluate choice of class pet.

Who Does the Assessing? How Is the Library Media Specialist Involved?

Traditionally, assessment has been the province of the classroom teacher. Teachers still retain the primary responsibility; however, the current literature on student learning reinforces the notion that assessment works best when the responsibility is shared (Kearney, 2000; Donham, 1998; AASL & AECT, 1998; Stiggins, 1997). There is a role in assessment for everyone beginning with the student.

Students

One of the primary goals of inquiry learning is to develop independent thinkers and problem solvers. Students must develop attitudes and habits of mind that include self-reflection and evaluation. They need to recognize and to strive for quality in their own performances. Self-assessment, therefore, is critical to the student's continuous growth as a learner.

Simmons (1994) connects reflection and self-assessment to the achievement of substantive understanding. If we want students to produce good work, they need to know in advance what good work looks like. This requires examining models and setting criteria to assess performance. Students, who reflect upon these criteria, develop deeper levels of understanding about the content and the learning process. As students become accustomed to using standards of quality to upgrade their performances, they gain a measure of control over their growth as independent learners.

Peers

Feedback from peers can add another dimension to the total assessment picture. When students work with partners or in small groups, they naturally engage in informal assessment. Conversations are interlaced with comments like "Why did you use this resource?" or "Why don't you add a picture here?" These remarks indicate that students are using certain criteria to assess and that they are willing to provide feedback.

We can maximize the effectiveness of peer assessment by teaching students how to provide responses that are descriptive and informative (Gregory, Cameron & Davies, 2000). The following example shows what the exchange might sound like when students work in small groups to provide feedback to one another. The students in this seventh grade scenario are helping a classmate develop an oral presentation on how volcanoes erupt.

> *Emily: I could hear you pretty well, but maybe you should slow down a little.*
> *Sam: I like the way you pointed to the lava when you explained how the volcano erupted.*
> *Jordan: I don't think you said what kind of a volcano it is. Did you?*
> *Kyle: That's right. I didn't. I'd better add that it's a composite volcano or the information won't be complete.*
> *Emily: I think maybe you should also explain what makes it a composite volcano.*
> *Kyle: You're right. I know where I can find that information.*

As the conversation shows, students can be very helpful in providing constructive feedback. The key is to create a non-threatening environment where students feel that they are helping rather than criticizing each other and where they view themselves as collaborators rather than as competitors.

Parents

The value of involving parents in the assessment process has been well documented in educational literature (Davies, 2000). Some of the following practices have been effective in engaging parents in the inquiry process:

Three-way-conferences that includes the student, parents, and teachers. These differ from traditional parent-teacher conferences in that the students take the lead role in informing parents about their progress. Using their process-folios as data, they explain the performance tasks and lay out evidence of their achievement. Parents are encouraged to participate in the conversation and to make comments and suggestions about the students' progress. The teacher serves as a facilitator, adding her perspective when it is warranted. The conference usually results in a new set of performance goals to which all parties agree.

Personal communication that solicits feedback. A short note from the child to his parents can focus attention on what is important about the project and solicit feedback from the parents. The note can be sent home with an invitation to a school event or it can be attached to the project itself. The examples below include a student's note to his parents and his parents' response.

Dear Mom and Dad,

Please come to our curriculum fair. It will be held in the library media center every day this week until 7 p.m.

My class studied the Age of Exploration and how it changed the world. I did a project on Ferdinand Magellan who was the first person to sail around the world. I wanted to explain why his exploration was so important.

When you look at my project, please notice my map where I drew his route and labeled the important places that he stopped at. Also take a look at my process-folio. You will see that I had to do a lot of work to make this project.

Your son,
Luke

Here is the response that Luke's parents attached to his project.

Dear Luke,

We were very pleased with your project on Magellan. The map was very informative. We knew that he had sailed around the world, but we didn't know his route. You did a good job of marking all the important places that he passed through on his journey.

One thing we are not sure about is why he is given credit for being the first to sail around the world when he actually died in the Philippines. Maybe that part of your report can be a little clearer.

Your process-folio showed us all the things that were involved in the project. We're happy that you are learning to be a researcher.

Love,
Mom and Dad

Teachers

The teachers' role is to orchestrate the entire assessment process by providing strategies and tools for self-assessment, peer assessment, and even parent assessment. Teachers use the assessment data from all sources to adjust instruction, to plan interventions, to modify the curriculum, and to evaluate students. They also use assessment information to confer with students and parents and to summarize data for use by administrators and policy makers.

Library Media Specialists

The question is not *whether* library media specialists should be involved in assessment but *when*, *how*, and *to what extent* they should participate in this crucial activity. Inquiry-based projects afford library media specialists an excellent opportunity to integrate the assessment of information literacy skills, which are fundamental to both inquiry and research. These skills include:

- Selecting an appropriate focus for investigation.
- Formulating research questions.
- Planning and executing a search strategy.
- Accessing information in print and electronic sources.
- Analyzing and selecting information that relate to the research questions.
- Taking notes that are accurate, relevant, and complete.
- Citing sources.
- Choosing an effective medium for sharing information.
- Organizing information for an effective presentation.
- Creating quality products and performances.

The library media specialist takes the lead in assessing parts of the process that she directly teaches (e.g., determining search strategies, accessing different types of resources, citing sources). In addition, she assists in designing assessment tools for parts of the process that may be conducted in the classroom and reinforced in the library (e.g., selecting a focus, formulating research questions, taking notes). She may also collaborate on product assessment.

Conclusion

Successful learning is not defined by what teachers and library media specialists do but rather by what the students are able to do (Guskey, 2003). If the ultimate goal of learning is understanding, assessment strategies must extend beyond one-dimensional tests administered at the end of a unit. The multi-faceted nature of inquiry learning makes it all the more imperative for assessment to encompass students' ability to use critical thinking and problem solving as well as research and communication skills to acquire content knowledge.

For students to move toward independence as learners, they need to understand what is expected of them and they must share ownership in self-monitoring their own progress. When teachers and library media specialists work with students on assessment, they help them to "confirm, consolidate, and integrate new knowledge" (Davies, 2000, pg. 6).

At the same time, assessment in the classroom and library media center informs the instructional team about what is working and where adjustments and modifications are needed. In brief, assessment is a central ingredient for student learning and for responsive teaching, not an optional one.

6 Connecting Information Searching and Inquiry

In chapter 4, we discussed the development of theme and problem-based units of study as two possible approaches to inquiry learning. In this chapter, we drill deeper into the teaching role of the library media specialist within these types of units and examine the building blocks for creating effective learning experiences for students.

How Do Information Search Process Models Support Inquiry?

A model or framework for the information search process defines the skills and competencies that learners need to master if they are to become effective locators, evaluators, and users of information. Grover and others (cited in Loertscher & Woolls, 2002) indicate that the use of these models has a positive impact on student achievement at all educational levels. They specifically point to the overall improvement in higher level thinking skills and the impact of the model on lower achieving students. In addition, they maintain that the use of models provides a vital context for collaborative planning and fosters the fuller involvement of library media specialists in the entire teaching and learning process.

There are many well-respected models available (e.g., Pappas & Tepe, 1997; Kuhlthau, 1994; Eisenberg & Berkowitz, 1990; Stripling & Pitts, 1988). Although there may be subtle distinctions among the various models, they all address the following critical elements:

- **Recognize the need to see the big picture.**
  Instruction begins with initiating or presearch activities intended to broaden students' understanding of a topic, an issue, or a problem.

- **Involve students in determining a focus for the research.**
  Students find a focus by narrowing the topic, writing a thesis or a statement of purpose, and developing questions to guide their investigations.

> ## This chapter:
> - Highlights the use of information search process models.
> - Stresses information literacy skills as thinking skills.
> - Outlines strategies to teach those skills.
> - Teaches key components of effective lessons.
> - Discusses meeting diverse student needs.
> - Underscores technology as tools for learning.

- **Address the need for planning the research and the presentation.**
  Students learn to select appropriate information sources, to plan search strategies, and to create effective plans for the presentation of knowledge.

- **Require students to collect and evaluate information from different sources.**
  Students learn the rudiments of accessing resources, evaluating information in terms of the research questions, taking notes, and citing sources.

- **Provide opportunities for students to organize and present their information.**
  Students present their knowledge for review by a real audience.

- **Recognize the critical role of assessment.**
  Ongoing assessment is fundamental to each model. Students reflect on their progress throughout their investigation and participate in assessing both their final product and their own learning process.

- **View the information search process as nonlinear.**
  Students go back and forth through this process as they discover the need for clarification, verification, and depth.

Many library media specialists have adopted one of these published models to frame their information literacy curriculum. Others have adapted concepts from these models and designed their own frameworks. For example, at Mililani Mauka Elementary in Hawaii (1995), the teachers and library media specialists devised a "My Search" process (Figure 6.1) that was a hybrid of other popular models.

Figure 6.1: Steps in the "My Search" Process

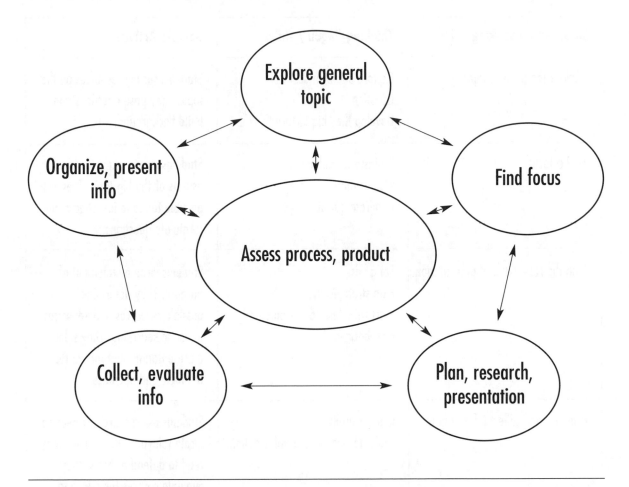

The Mililani team envisioned this as a model that could grow with the students. For example, the wording might be simplified for the very youngest children. As students progressed through the grade levels, the steps of the model could be expanded or deepened by adding more sophisticated layers of skills. Over the years, the team discovered that having this model provided a consistent framework across grade levels for the information search process regardless of the theme or problem being studied.

How Does the Information Search Process Support Inquiry Learning?

In chapter 1 we discussed thinking skills that might be taught in both the classroom and the library media center. Here we connect thinking skills more directly with an information literacy model and provide examples of how students might actually demonstrate these skills in the course of an information-related project (Figure 6.2).

Figure 6.2: Linking Information Search Skills with Skills in Thinking and Inquiry

Information seeking skills	Thinking/inquiry skills	Sample Activities
Explore the general topic.	Explore and browse. Question. Develop the "big picture."	Students survey resources on the topic. They pose questions and build background.
Find a focus.	Brainstorm and list. Web or map. Generate questions.	Students create maps to show aspects of the big topic. They list possible topics to investigate and formulate questions.
Plan the research and presentation.	Set goals. Plan strategically. Start with desired outcome and plan backward.	Students write a statement of purpose. They determine possible resources and keywords to use in searching. They select a presentation appropriate for the topic and audience.
Evaluate and collect information.	Read critically. Evaluate relevance of information.	Students use a search strategy to locate relevant information. They read to defend a thesis. They evaluate sources for relevancy, accuracy, and currency. They cite sources.
Organize and present information.	Analyze and synthesize information. Communicate effectively.	Students organize their information for an effective presentation. They create a draft, edit and revise, practice, adjust, and present.
Assess the process and product.	Recognize quality. Reflect. Make adjustments.	Students determine criteria for each step in the process. They reflect on what they are learning and how they are feeling. They make adjustments based on feedback.

Which Instructional Strategies Work Best?

Effective learning is a holistic experience. It involves "an interplay of thoughts, feelings, and actions" (Kuhlthau, n.d.). In this learner-focused approach, motivation and challenge are critical ingredients (Pappas & Tepe, 2002). The success of an entire project often hinges on the degree to which students "buy in" to the learning experience. All of this indicates that teachers and library media specialists need to design instructional activities that have the potential to involve students in the task of learning. Although different strategies may be used to introduce various steps in the process, there are certain elements common in all of these approaches. They include:

- A challenging task that requires critical or creative thinking.
- Opportunities for students to interact as they share ideas or complete a task.
- Active involvement by all members of the group.
- A verifiable outcome that builds toward the achievement of goals.

Figure 6.3 presents examples of strategies that engage students in hands-on and intellectually stimulating tasks.

Not all of these strategies are suitable for a given unit of study; deciding which learning experiences will best fit the situation is a critical part of the curriculum planning process. The overarching focus is how effectively a particular strategy might involve students in the inquiry process. Critical questions to ask include:

- Is the strategy age-appropriate?
- Does the strategy provide for active engagement and feedback?
- How much experience have these students had with each phase of the information search process?
- How familiar are they with the topic or problem being studied?
- How much time is available?
- Who will take the lead in providing the instruction?
- Are sufficient resources available?

Figure 6.3: Instructional Strategies for Teaching the Information Search Process

Steps in the process	Instructional strategies
Explore the general topic	• **Read-in** — Use a four-step process to get an overview of the topic. • **Video** — Show a video that introduces the problem or the "big picture." • **Internet tour** — Engage in an Internet tour of sites dealing with the general topic. • **Field trip** — Visit a museum, a natural site, or other places in the local community that highlight a problem or spark interest.
Find a focus	• **Brainstorming session** — Work in small groups to brainstorm aspects of the problem or issue. • **Webbing** — Create webs or concept maps showing different ways of approaching the topic. • **Writing a thesis or statement of purpose** — Create statements identifying which aspects of the problem students will research and for what purpose (e.g., "In my presentation I will compare the mythology of ancient Greece and ancient Rome"). • **K-W-L chart** — List what they know about the problem or issue and what they want to find out. After the research is completed, they list the things they have learned. • **Forming critical questions** — Use the K-W-L chart to write questions that will guide the research.
Plan the research and presentation	• **Backward planning** — Start by clearly defining the expected outcomes for a project. Students devise plans of action with the desired goals in mind. Their plans include benchmarks, tasks, and time lines. • **Goal setting** — Set personal goals for their projects. Students put in writing what aspect of the problem they will be researching, how it will be presented, and what level of quality they will aim for. • **Determining a search strategy** — Consider all the resources both within and outside the school and select those most likely to help answer the questions. Also determine the keywords that will be used to search print and electronic resources.
Evaluate and collect information	• **Using a pathfinder** — Explore resources that might be relevant by using a pathfinder. Teachers, the media specialist, and more experienced peers coach students as they access resources. Prior to the search, criteria are established for evaluating the appropriateness of information retrieved.

Figure 6.3 *continued*

Steps in the process	Instructional strategies
	• **Skimming and scanning**—Skim and scan using textual aids to locate specific information.
	• **Reading for information**—Interpret the text in terms of the information sought. Analyze details used to present an argument, look for bias, and draw inferences supported by facts. From the entire text, extract the information needed to support a thesis or answer a research question.
	• **Note taking**—Set criteria for effective notes. The teacher or library media specialist models the process of taking good notes from various sources. Compare notes against established criteria.
Organize and present information	• **Planning to present**—Review and modify action plans before planning a final presentation. Students consider the content, the audience, and the purpose of the presentation.
	• **Establishing assessment criteria**—Determine assessment criteria. These criteria serve as guides for students working on presentations.
	• **Organizing notes**—Use the thesis or statement of purpose as an anchor for organizing notes.
	• **Drafting, assessing, revising**—Engage in a cyclical process of drafting, assessing, and revising. Use criteria to self-assess presentations and consider feedback from teachers and peers. Students revise and adjust as they work toward performance criteria.
Assess the process and product	• **Brainstorming assessment criteria**—Set criteria for each step in the process, i.e., selecting a topic, developing research questions, writing good notes, presenting the information.
	• **Self-monitoring**—Use rubrics, checklists, and rating scales to monitor self-progress.
	• **Conferencing**—Initiate conferences with teachers and library edia specialists as needed.
	• **Reflecting**—Keep research logs in which students reflect upon what they learn, the questions they have, the problems they encounter, and how they plan to proceed.

How Do We Facilitate the Learning?

The information search process calls for a complex array of skills and understandings. To help students gain proficiency in these areas, library media specialists and teachers must have a repertoire of teaching strategies to incorporate into their units of study. Regardless of the strategy used, however, certain elements of sound teaching must be reflected in these learning experiences (Allen, 1998; Wiggins & McTighe, 1998; Perkins, 1992). They include:

- **Direct instruction**
  Students need clear information about the task at hand. They need to know the objectives of the lesson or activity and the standards that will be used to assess performance.
- **Modeling**
  Students need to see examples of what is expected. If the end result of a lesson is a product, samples of student products are presented and critiqued. When a skill (such as note taking) is the target of the lesson, the teacher or library media specialist models the process by interacting with students in a "think aloud" process.
- **Interaction**
  Students need to converse with their teachers and peers as a means of clarifying thinking, exchanging ideas, and providing instructional support. Interaction is achieved through cooperative learning groups, two-way journals, and conferences. Additional opportunities for interaction can be woven into the instruction through "think-pair-share" strategies where students first think of a response, which they exchange with a partner and later share with the whole group.
- **Guided practice**
  Students must practice the skills that have been presented. Guided practice calls for teachers to supplement direct instruction with facilitation or coaching. This is especially important when students are learning complex skills such as reading for information or taking notes. It is also an effective strategy for introducing students to new technologies.
- **Independent practice**
  Students also need to reinforce a skill. Complex tasks like evaluating information, taking notes, or planning a presentation must be practiced in different contexts for confidence and proficiency to develop.
- **Feedback and continual assessment**
  Descriptive feedback is critical for improvement. Very often this feedback is in the form of questions posed by instructors and peers that provoke students to assess their work. The goal of descriptive feedback is continual adjustment and improvement.

How might these various strategies and components of effective learning come together in a unit of study?

Figure 6.4 provides one example of how the library media specialist and teacher might embed these strategies and elements in an actual unit of study. This example is based on the work of a sixth grade class at Mililani Mauka Elementary that studied the theme of "change over time." The first unit focused on ancient civilizations and the second on modern cultures. After investigating the question, "What defines a civilization?" students selected an ancient civilization to research. Later in the school year, they studied the same part of the world but in the modern era. Finally, they synthesized their information by returning to the essential question, "How do civilizations change over time?"

What if a lesson doesn't work?

No strategy works for all students and in all situations. When our assessment indicates that students are not achieving the desired learning outcomes, we might ask ourselves the following critical questions:

- Were the goals clearly stated?
- Were models provided so students knew what was expected?
- Were students given an opportunity to interact among themselves and with their instructors so that directions could be clarified and questions addressed?
- Were opportunities provided for guided practice under the direct supervision of instructors?
- Was the guided practice accompanied by informative feedback focused on improvement rather than criticism?
- Were students encouraged to assess their performance using established criteria?

In spite of our best efforts, we often find that assessment data pinpoint areas where we might improve instructional delivery. When this happens, we may need to re-teach the skill or process using a different approach. In the Mililani Mauka example, several sixth graders, who participated in the read-in, indicated in their reflection journals that they needed more information about ancient civilizations before choosing a topic to research. One student said:

> The read-in was fun. I enjoyed the books especially the one about Egyptian mummies. I learned a lot of things I didn't know before, like how they took out the insides and drained the blood before they made the mummy. I looked at other civilizations, too. I thought the Romans were pretty cool. Maybe I could research the coliseum [sic]. Besides those two, I still don't know too much about other ancient civilizations. I think I need to look at more books before I decide.

After reading many journal entries similar to this one, the teacher and library media specialist decided to extend the exploration phase using a video that provided an overview of the ancient world. They also scheduled time in the computer lab to take students on an Internet tour of museums of ancient history.

Figure 6.4: Examples of Alignment of Information Search Process, Instructional Strategies, and Elements of Effective Teaching

1. Explore the general topic.

Instructional strategies	Elements of effective teaching
• **Read-in**	**Direct instruction/modeling** • The library media specialist (LMS) explains the purpose of the read-in — to explore the topic of ancient civilizations and to become familiar with resources about the topic. • The structure of the read-in is presented: (1) select something to read, (2) read for 5-10 minutes, (3) write a new fact or idea that you learned about ancient civilizations, (4) share something interesting. • The teacher or LMS models each step in the process so students know what to do and how to do it. **Interaction** • Students work in cooperative groups. • Students practice attentive listening and participate fully in the session. **Guided practice/feedback** • Teachers and LMS facilitate each step in the process to ensure full participation and attention to goals. **Independent practice** • The 4-step activity is repeated three times during the read-in.

2. Find a focus.

Instructional strategies	Elements of effective teaching
• **Webbing** • **Writing research questions** • **Writing a statement of purpose**	**Direct instruction/modeling** • Teacher presents an overview of the unit, including objectives, performance standards, and a time line. • Teacher also provides specific directions for writing a statement of purpose. • Teacher provides sample statements of purpose (e.g., "In my presentation I will explain how the pyramids of Egypt were built"). • Teacher uses the think-aloud process to model how to write questions. This involves thinking aloud about the topic and voicing some of the questions that come to mind. For example:

Figure 6.4 *continued*

—What do I know about it?

—Why is it important or interesting?

—How is it made?

—How does it relate to the big topic?

Interaction

Students work in small groups to:

- Create a web showing components that define a civilization.
- Discuss these various components.
- Determine criteria for relevant questions.

Guided practice/feedback

- Students practice writing questions and statements of purpose.
- Teacher and LMS circulate among student groups to provide direction and feedback.

Independent practice/feedback

- Students use feedback to revise and adjust their selection of topics, their research questions, and their statements of purpose.

3. Plan the research and the presentation.

Instructional strategies	Elements of effective teaching
• **Backward planning** • **Planning a search strategy**	**Direct instruction** • Teacher walks students through the process of determining how to present information, breaking down the steps leading up to presentation, and setting a tentative time line. **Modeling** • Teacher and LMS provide models of effective presentations. • LMS shares a template detailing the components of the research action plan. • LMS demonstrates possible search strategies. **Guided practice/feedback** • Students use templates to work out the details of their action plans. Teacher facilitates and provides feedback. • Students work on search strategies. Teacher and LMS provide feedback. **Independent practice/feedback** • Students adjust plans as they work.

Figure 6.4 *continued*

4. Evaluate and collect information.

Instructional strategies	Elements of effective teaching
• **Reading for information** • **Note taking**	**Direct instruction/modeling** • Teacher demonstrates the process of reading and taking notes from various resources. **Interaction** • Students work in groups to brainstorm criteria for effective notes. **Guided practice/feedback** • Teacher and LMS facilitate as students access, evaluate, and retrieve information. • Teacher and LMS help students to assess their notes based upon criteria established. **Independent practice** • Students repeat the process as they seek information using various resources.

5. Organize and present information.

Instructional strategies	Elements of effective teaching
• **Review/revise presentation plan** • **Organize notes** • **Draft, assess, revise**	**Direct instruction** • Teacher and LMS review the purpose of the action plan and the ultimate goal of the project—to address the essential question: How do civilizations change over time? **Guided practice/feedback** • Students organize notes, compose drafts, and seek feedback from teachers and peers. • Students use feedback to revise presentations. • Students review presentation plans, confer with teams and instructors, and make adjustments as needed.

Figure 6.4 *continued*

6. Assess the process and product.

Instructional strategies	Elements of effective teaching
• **Brainstorming criteria** • **Using rubrics** • **Reflecting** • **Conferencing**	**Interaction** • Students and instructors establish criteria and design rubrics to assess learning. **Guided practice** • Students use rubrics to prepare presentations. **Feedback** • Students solicit feedback through reflection journals. • Students initiate conferences, as they need assistance.

How Are Diverse Student Needs and Abilities Addressed?

The mixed-ability class is a reality in today's schools. There may be students who read three or four grades levels above the norm and those who barely read at all. Some youngsters may come from homes where English is not the primary language. Others may have physical or mental disabilities that interfere with learning, and still others may be so overwhelmed by the effects of poverty or neglect that school is only a sidebar in their lives. As educators we are responsible for teaching them all. How to accomplish this is a major challenge. Being able to accommodate different needs is a critical consideration whether teaching occurs in the classroom or in the library media center. According to Tomlinson (1995), differentiated instruction has several important characteristics:

- Students are given a variety of ways to explore the curriculum.
- Teachers provide a variety of activities and processes aimed at helping students use information to create their own personal knowledge.
- Students have a variety of choices for presenting information or sharing knowledge.

Notice that the keyword here is "variety." Since one size does not fit all, educators must possess a repertoire of strategies to meet the diverse needs of students. In the sixth grade unit described in this chapter, this is how instruction was differentiated for four students.

Example 1: Max and Henry

Max was a special needs student who read at a third grade level. He and Henry, another student with reading difficulties, decided to research the pyramids of Egypt. In their statement of purpose the boys said they would "build a pyramid to scale and explain how the ancient Egyptians were able to do this." Their research questions included the following:

- What did a pyramid look like?
- What were the dimensions of a pyramid?
- What materials were used to build it?
- How did they build it?
- Who did the work?

Here is how Jane, a gifted student in the class, addressed the same assignment.

Example 2: Jane

Jane also wanted to research the pyramids of Egypt. In her statement of purpose she indicated that she would prepare a multimedia presentation that examined what the pyramids reflected about Egyptian society. Her research questions included the following:

- Who built the pyramids?
- Why were pyramids built?
- Who was buried in the pyramids?
- How was a body prepared for burial?
- What does this say about how Egyptians viewed the afterlife?
- By studying the pyramids, what lessons can we learn about Egyptian society?

Finally, consider how Rosa Maria, a recent arrival from the Philippines, approached this assignment.

Example 3: Rosa

At home Rosa spoke a Filipino dialect. Because she came from a traditional educational system in the Philippines, she was uneasy with the student-centered approaches used in the inquiry environment. She was reticent about participating in whole class discussions so the small learning groups provided the support she needed to be successful. Her peers explained procedures, interpreted text, and coached her through the process. Rosa chose the Philippines as her research focus. Her plan was to create a display board showing how the ancient people lived. The questions she wanted to explore were as follows:

- Who were the original inhabitants of the Philippines?
- How did these people live?
- What kind of clothing did they wear?
- How did they build their homes?
- What did they eat?
- What were some of their customs and beliefs?

Max and Henry

As expected, the presentations made by these students were very different. Max and Henry selected a very concrete topic to research and present. Before approving their choice, the teacher, Mr. Young, checked with the library media specialist to see if the central collection had easy reading material that would be accessible to them. To focus their search for information, Max and his partner posed questions that would help them to achieve their goals. For these students the teacher felt that a reliance on questions beginning with who and what was an appropriate starting point. However, he also used cueing techniques to elicit more details from the students. Here is part of a conversation that took place when the teacher was reviewing Max's notes on who built the pyramids:

> Teacher: Max, I agree that the Egyptians built the pyramids but which Egyptians are you talking about? Did the Pharaoh help to build them?
> Max (looking at a book on the topic): Oh, it says that it was the lower class or the laborers and slaves helped them.

At the end, Max, wrote the following reflection:

> Henry and me had a lot of fun making the pyramid. We found a book that had a diagram of a real pyramid that showed the measurements, and Mr. Young, our teacher, helped us to make a scale drawing. We used cardboard for the model. Then we covered it with clay. It was hard, but not as hard as it was for the Egyptian slaves.

Jane

Although Jane also chose to focus her research on the pyramids, she approached the topic from another perspective. Jane was encouraged by her teacher and the library media specialist to select a more challenging performance task and to ask questions that would require an in-depth interpretation of the information. In preparing her multimedia presentation, Jane sought assistance from the school's technology coordinator as well as the expertise of her more technology-oriented peers. Her presentation extended beyond the pyramids to provide a glimpse into many facets of life in ancient Egypt. It proved to be a valuable resource for all of the students in the project. This is what she has to say about the project:

> I was really upset when Mr. Young said that I couldn't build a pyramid. It didn't seem fair since Max and Henry got to build one. But I have to admit that I learned a lot by doing the multimedia project. It was a good way to show everything I learned about the Egyptians, not just about the pyramids. I had to spend a lot of recesses working on the project. It's a good thing Mr. Aki, the technology coordinator, helped me. I also got a lot of help from my classmates, Chris and Megan. In the end I think the multimedia show was the best choice for a project because I got to show what a pyramid looked like and to explain how it was built and how it related to the beliefs of the Egyptians, especially their ideas about the afterlife.

Rosa

The challenges facing Rosa were quite different from the other students. Although she was fairly advanced in her ability to decode English text, she had little experience with the reading skills needed to locate, interpret, and apply information. In addition to the language barrier, she was not familiar with the constructivist approach to learning being used in this classroom. Luckily, Rosa found support in the cooperative learning groups that were integral to the inquiry process. She also selected a focus of genuine personal interest. In her log, she reflected:

> I thought I wouldn't like research. I hate it when I don't know what to do. I'm glad that Mari and Ken are in my group. When I don't understand what the teacher means, they always explain it to me…. I'm glad I got to pick my own topic. Mom and Dad said it's good that I am learning about my homeland. They are going to take me to the library downtown to get more information. I like to draw so Mr. Young said that would be a good way for me to show what I learned. I think I'll make a display board like the one he showed the class.

The experiences of these students indicate that there are ways to meet the needs of a diverse group of youngsters in an inquiry-learning environment. This type of accommodation requires knowledge of the students and their needs, knowledge of the topic and its complexities, and knowledge of the skills embedded in the information search process.

How Might Technology Enhance Student Learning?

Technology has revolutionized how teachers teach and students learn. Today's children have the wisdom of the world literally at their fingertips. Consider how technology enhanced both teaching and learning in the following project.

Technology in a science project

A high school science class investigated the issue of sustainable agriculture and the importance of soil conservation. They began their study with a trip via the Internet to gather background information on soil composition in different parts of the U.S. They then worked in groups to brainstorm what they knew about soil composition and different types of soil. They fashioned their study around "How does soil in our area affect our agriculture? What can be done to protect or improve our agriculture?" Some of their questions were as follows:

- What are the basic types of soil?
- How does soil affect the growth and development of plants?
- How do farmers work with soil to improve productivity?
- What can be done to prevent soil deterioration?

Students established teams to find answers to their questions. Following the steps in the information search process, they used a variety of print and electronic resources to locate information. Through e-mail and videoconferences, they contacted local agricultural and geological experts for information. One team volunteered to create a database summarizing the effects of natural and human impact on soil composition. Another team created a PowerPoint presentation focusing on the issue of soil conservation and suggesting ways to deal with it. The remaining teams designed multimedia presentations that included links to other Web sites on the issue. These presentations were shared at an environmental fair staged at a local shopping mall.

In this project, students were engaged in a problem-based project on sustainable agriculture. To accomplish their objectives, students were deeply involved in the information search process. They made their own decisions about questions to ask, topics to research, and the design of their presentations. At the same time, they were addressing many of the standards outlined in educational technology (International Society for Technology in Education, n.d.). Figure 6.5 captures this information.

Figure 6.5: Example of Technology Standards Addressed in a Unit

Categories of technology standards	Applications in the unit
Basic operations and concepts	Students used the Internet and other technologies to retrieve, manipulate, and download information. This required application of basic Web searching skills and some knowledge of how these systems operate.
Social, ethical, and human issues	Students developed an appreciation of technology as a tool for lifelong learning. They followed school policies concerning the use of technology. They worked in teams to accomplish a common purpose. They acknowledged the information sources used in their presentations.
Technology productivity tools	Students learned the skills needed to create an effective presentation. Their products and performances met standards for accuracy, completeness, and creativity.
Technology communication tools	Students used e-mail to interact with experts outside the school. They used word processing skills to effectively communicate their knowledge with a mass audience. They enhanced their presentations with appropriate visual and audio features.
Technology research tools	Students used the online catalog, electronic encyclopedias, magazine databases, and other Web resources to locate, evaluate, and retrieve information.

Could this unit have been done two decades ago? The answer might be a qualified "yes." Surely the library collection included books on the topic. These could have been supplemented with articles from *National Geographic* and similar magazines. The teachers might have been able to arrange for a geologist or agricultural extension agent from the local university to speak to the class about the problem. The students could have written a report or maybe even done a hands-on project about the issue. However, if you compare this scenario with the richness and depth of experience provided through the use of appropriate technologies, there can be no doubt that today's learners have benefited from the technological revolution.

What challenges accompany the introduction of technology?

To effectively use the different technologies, students must be able to:

- Articulate the information needed as clearly as possible.
- Understand the function of each type of technology.
- Identify appropriate resources to search.
- Execute a search strategy.
- Read and evaluate the information located.
- Evaluate Web sites for authority, timeliness, accuracy, and relevance.
- Select information to download with reference to research questions.
- Print selected text.
- Follow e-mail protocols for online communication.
- Understand the purpose and function of selected software programs, i.e., databases, multimedia, and presentation software.
- Use software tools to create effective presentations.

Some of these skills involve the physical manipulation of technological resources. Students quickly learn these skills when teachers or peers coach them through a task. In contrast, abilities such as reading for information and evaluating Web sites are much more difficult for students to acquire. Direct instruction and repeated opportunities for guided practice are needed for students to acquire these critical thinking skills.

With the ever-increasing volume of information, the instructional focus has shifted from finding information to managing the information found. Whereas in the past we taught students how to access and use a comparatively limited range of print and nonprint resources, the explosion of the Internet as an information provider brings a new set of challenges for library media specialists. Working with college students, Repman and Carlson (2002) maintain that learners need to develop Web searching skills and strategies in a systematic way. This includes understanding something about the structure of the Internet and the use of different search tools to narrow or broaden searches.

Students need guidelines for filtering the information available on the Internet. These guidelines are acquired when instructional practices involve students in processes like brainstorming and selecting criteria for evaluating Web sites. By converting criteria into guiding questions, students learn to use the Internet efficiently and effectively. Figure 6.6 provides examples of questions used by students as they evaluate Web sites.

Conclusion

Integrating information literacy skills into inquiry learning projects requires acquiring a toolkit of strategies that engage and motivate students. It also challenges teachers and library media specialists to revisit their lessons and to ask themselves the following questions: Are my goals clearly identified for the students? Are the tasks and activities carefully scaffolded so that my students move from guided practice to more independent learning? Am I sensitive to the diverse range of students in my class? Have I shaped the learning experience to meet their unique needs? Am I incorporating technology as a tool for deeper learning? To the degree that we effectively deal with these issues in our teaching, we also successfully help young learners to achieve their goals.

Figure 6.6: Questions Used to Evaluate Web Sites

Evaluative criteria	Guiding questions
Authority	Who created this Web site? Is the person or organization an authority in this field?
Accuracy	Does the content appear to be accurate? Are sources of information cited?
Relevance	Does the information relate to my topic? Does it help to answer my questions?
Timeliness	How recent is the information? Is currency important to my research focus?
Organization	Does the design of the Web page help me to read and understand the content? Are graphics provided to help explain the concepts?
Readability	Can I read and understand the text?

7 Profile of an Elementary School Project

In the preceding chapters, we discussed how inquiry learning develops from larger themes as well as from issues and problems. We also described possible tools to assess learning and explained how units and lessons evolve from principles of effective teaching and learning. In chapters 7 through 9, we bring the pieces together in descriptions of projects at the elementary, middle, and high school levels.

In this chapter, we highlight a first grade project on animal adaptation. We have organized the profile in a template format under the following components:

- Summary of project.
- Learner goals.
- Culminating product or performance.
- Essential questions.
- Standards addressed.
- Assessment criteria and methods.
- Resources.
- Teaching strategies and procedures.

Samples of graphic organizers are also included at the end of each profile. We have not specified the number of instructional sessions or the amount of time needed for the projects since these will vary according to instructional schedules as well as student readiness in different classrooms. In addition, although we have given examples of how responsibilities might be shared among instructors, actual assignments will depend on the strengths and skills of the particular team members involved.

Grade 2—Animal adaptation

Summary of project

Theme or issue: Animal adaptation.

Grade level or course: Grade 2, interdisciplinary.

Duration of project: Six to eight weeks.

Students visit the local zoo and return with many questions about where these animals originally came from and what the animals' lives would be like if they were back in their real homes. They work with fourth grade students, who serve as "research buddies," to locate and retrieve information on various animals. The process helps the older students to take responsibility for the younger children. The second graders benefit from the individualized attention provided by the older students.

Learner goals

Content Goals
Students will demonstrate knowledge of the following:
- Diversity of life within a habitat.
- Relationship between all living things in a habitat.
- Basic needs of animals—food, water, air, protection.
- Unique characteristics of animals related to survival in a habitat.
- Behaviors needed to survive in a habitat.

Process Goals
Students will demonstrate an ability to
- Collect, organize, and use information to generate new knowledge.
- Use the reading process to locate, interpret, and record information that answers research questions.
- Use the writing process to present information about the topic.
- Use the speaking and listening processes to communicate ideas.
- Present information creatively and effectively.

Culminating product or performance

Students create a habitat in the classroom. They make masks of the animals and write books about the animals for the classroom habitat library. The book provides information about the animal itself, what it eats, how it behaves, and how it survives in the habitat. It also includes illustrations of the habitat and the plants and animals that live in it. At the end of the unit the class hosts a habitat fair for other first grade classes where students share what they have produced. Parents are also invited.

Essential questions

- What plants and animals live in the habitat?
- What do all plants and animals need to survive?
- How does the habitat help plants and animals to meet their needs?
- What problems do animals have surviving in the habitat?
- What body parts and behaviors help animals to survive?

Standards addressed

Science Standards

Science Content Standard C: Life Science
As a result of activities in grades K-4, all students should develop understanding of:
- The characteristics of organisms.
- Life cycles of organisms.
- Organisms and environments.

Source: National Academy of Sciences. (n.d.). *National science education standards, Chapter 6: Content standard 3: The characteristics of organisms*. Retrieved April 2, 2003, from <http://www.nap.edu/readingroom/books/nses/html/6d.html>

School-level science benchmarks for grade 1
Students will demonstrate understanding of the following concepts:
- Plants and animals meet their needs in different ways.
- Plants and animals inhabit different kinds of environments.
- Animals need food, water, and air to survive.
- Animals have different structures that help them to adapt to life in different habitats.
- Animal behavior is related to survival in a particular habitat.

Standards addressed (continued)

Language Arts Standards

Language Arts Standards: Oral communication
- Students will use strategies within speaking and listening processes to construct and communicate meaning.

Language Arts Standards: Reading
- Students will read a range of literary and informative texts for a variety of purposes.
- Students will use strategies within the reading process to construct meaning.

Language Arts Standards: Writing
- Students will write using various forms to communicate for a variety of purposes and audiences.
- Students will use writing processes and strategies to construct meaning and communicate effectively.

Source: Hawaii Department of Education. (n.d.). *Hawaii content and performance standards: Language arts content standards*. Retrieved April 1, 2003, from <http://doe.k12.hi.us/standards/hcps.htm>

Information Literacy Standards

Standard 1: The student who is information literate accesses information efficiently and effectively.

Standard 3: The student who is information literate uses information accurately and creatively.

Standard 9: The student who contributes positively to the learning community and to society is information literate and participates effectively in groups to pursue and generate information.

Source: From *Information Power: Building Partnerships for Learning* by American Association of School Librarians and Association for Educational Communications and Technology. ©1998. American Library Association and Association for Educational Communications and Technology. Reprinted by permission of the American Library Association.

Assessment

Criteria	Methods
Content skills Students will demonstrate knowledge of: • Concept of a habitat. • Diversity of life within a habitat. • Basic needs of animals. • How animals adapt to satisfy needs. • Structures and behaviors developed by animals to survive in a habitat. **Process skills** Students will demonstrate an ability to: • Work cooperatively to share information and explore ideas. • Skim and scan for information. • Locate information that answers research questions. • Interpret information in terms of the questions to be answered. • Focus writing around the main idea. • Support the main idea with details. • Write in complete sentences. • Organize sentences into paragraphs. • Draw pictures that clarify the ideas in the writing. **Information skills process** • Choose a topic to research. • Ask questions to guide the research. • Make a web to organize the search for information. • Access and retrieve information from a variety of resources. • Take notes that answer the questions. • Analyze and organize the notes. • Write from the notes. • Present information both visually and in writing.	**I CAN statements** These statements define expectations in language clearly understood by students. From these statements, a checklist is developed to guide them through the process. Examples: • I can explain why different animals live in different habitats. • I can explain how different body parts and behaviors help animals to survive. • I can draw a picture of the habitat that shows the plants and animals that live there. • I can make a web showing what I need to find out about my animal. • I can find information about my topic in books, encyclopedias, and the Internet. • I can take notes that answer my research questions. • I can use my notes to write about my animal. • I can write in complete sentences. • I can organize sentences into paragraphs. **Learning logs** Students keep logs where they reflect on the process. **Informal checking** T and LMS focus on how students are meeting the criteria. **Examination of student work** T and LMS examine students' webs, notes, and drafts on an ongoing basis so that adjustments can be made.

Possible Resources

Internet Resources

- *Yahooligans* at <www.yahooligans.com>
  Choose "Animals" and search by category or keyword.
- *Searchasaurus* at <www.epnet.com/school/k12search2.asp>
  Choose "Primary Search" for full text magazine articles or go to the "Animal Encyclopedia."
- *Enchanted Learning* at <www.enchantedlearning.com>
  Choose "Biomes" for information about the habitat. Use "Animal Printouts" for labels, information, and pictures to color.
- *Animal Information Database* at <www.seaworld.org/AnimalBytes/animal_bytes.html>
  Choose "Animal Bytes" and locate animals within categories.
- *National Geographic Creature Features* at <www.nationalgeographic.com/kids/creatures_features>
  Explore buttons for quick facts, video, games, and more.

Additional Resources

- Informational books, videos, and DVDs from the library media center are located using the school's OPAC.
- Children's magazines: *Zoobooks*, *National Geographic Kids*, *Your Big Backyard*.
- Print encyclopedias: *Marshall Cavendish's Wildlife and Plants of the World*.
- CD ROM encyclopedias: *2003 World Book* CD-ROM (Windows or Mac).

Strategies and procedures

T = teacher
LMS = library media specialist

1. Generate interest, curiosity

Teaching and learning strategies: Web exploration; predicting, reading, and validating.

T/LMS	Students	Assessment
Web exploring (T): Take students on an Internet field trip to explore how animals survive in different environments. ("Animal Adaptation," at <http://library.thinkquest.org/J001644F/default.htm>) Teach technology skills as needed, e.g., using the mouse to click on buttons. **Predicting, reading, and validating (T):** Ask students to predict where each animal lives before they access information. Have them validate their predictions. Ask questions to focus on the concept of a habitat: ● Where does the polar bear live? ● What does he eat? ● How does he survive? Have students define a habitat. Write responses on a chart.	**Web exploring:** Students explore a Web site to examine how different species survive in their environments. **Predicting:** As they explore the Web site, they predict where animals live and give reasons for their predictions. **Reading and validating:** They also: ● Skim the article to find information. ● Use the mouse to scroll through the article and to point to the information that answers a question. ● Use the "back" button to return to the home page. Work with a partner to say what a habitat is. Share their ideas with the class.	**Informal checking:** Are students: ● Selecting the right icon? ● Using the mouse to skim the article for keywords that answer questions? ● Using the "back" button to return to the main screen? Ask questions to encourage deeper understanding, for example: ● Why does the skunk have a strong smell? ● Why are polar bears white and grizzly bears brown? ● How does the toucan use its big bill? **Journal prompts:** ● What is a habitat? ● What kinds of habitats are there? ● Why is the habitat important to an animal?

2. Explore the theme or problem

Teaching and learning strategies: shared reading and viewing, think-pair-share.

T/LMS	Students	Assessment
Shared reading/viewing (T/LMS): Read or share a variety of fiction and nonfiction books that show animals living and surviving in different habitats. Examples include: • *Crinkleroot's Guide to Knowing Animal Habitats* by Jim Arnosky. Aladdin Library, 2000. • *An Elephant Never Forgets Its Snorkel: How Animals Survive Without Tools and Gadgets*, by Lisa Gollin Evans. Crown Publishing, 1992. Show videos dealing with different habitats. Examples include National Geographic's *Really Wild Animal* video series. Focus the discussion by asking questions like: • What kinds of animals live in the habitat? • What do they need to survive? • What problems do these animals have? • How do they adapt to overcome their problems?	Think-pair-share: Students demonstrate comprehension through participation in the Think-Pair-Share process: **THINK** about the question and how it can be answered. **PAIR** up with a partner to exchange ideas. **SHARE** your ideas with the class. They draw pictures of the habitats presented and include the plant and animal life native to the environment. They write sentences telling the name of the habitat and something interesting about it. Students create a word wall in the classroom and add the names of animals encountered through reading, listening, and viewing.	**Informal checking:** Are students: • Focusing on the story? • Giving thoughtful consideration to the question? • Exchanging ideas with a partner? • Responding appropriately, giving reasons for their responses? • Sharing ideas with the class? **Examination of student work:** Check that the picture is an accurate depiction of the habitat in terms of: • Terrain (grasslands, jungle, desert, etc.). • Plants (specificity and variety of plant life). • Animals (specificity and variety of animal life). • Indications of weather conditions. **I CAN statements:** • Draw a picture of the habitat and show the plants and animals that live there. • Write something interesting about the habitat. • Share what I write.

3. Generate questions, predictions

Teaching and learning strategies: questioning, predicting.

T/LMS	Students	Assessment
Generating questions (T): Encourage students to ask questions that they have about habitats in general. Post the questions for future reference. Questions might include: • What kinds of plants and animals live in this environment? • What do they need to live? • How do they get food? Water? Air? • How do animals protect themselves? • How do animals adapt to difficult environments like the polar regions or the desert? **Predicting (T/LMS):** Introduce a matching game related to animal homes in which students predict where the animals will live.	**Generating questions:** Students work with a partner to first say and then write questions about animal habitats. Fourth grade buddies assist with spelling. Each pair shares their best question and these are posted on the board to be addressed throughout the unit. **Predicting:** They divide into groups to create posters depicting different habitats (desert, rain forest, temperate forest, woodland, etc.) They place posters around the room for all to use. Students cut out pictures of animals and plants from magazines and predict which habitat the animal might live in. After review and discussion, they paste the animals onto the appropriate poster.	**Informal checking:** Are students: • Posing questions that indicate an understanding of the "big picture"? • Raising other pertinent questions? As students place animals on the habitat poster, ask questions to see if they have made thoughtful predictions: • Why do you think it lives here? • What will it eat? • How will it get water? • Who might be its enemies? **I CAN statements:** • Write questions about my animal and the habitat it lives in.

4. Identify a focus

Teaching and learning strategies: selecting an animal to research, webbing.

T/LMS	Students	Assessment
Selecting an animal (T/LMS): Have students select animals to research. Refer to the "Word Wall" for a list of animals in the habitat. Play "Twenty questions" to practice asking questions that will apply to any animal. LMS chooses an animal, and students ask questions until they guess who it is. **Webbing (T/LMS):** Help the class create a web that addresses the basic needs of all animals and includes description, food and water, behavior, and other elements related to adaptation. ***(See Figure 7.1. Web for animal adaptation)***	**Selecting an animal:** Students think of three animals they would like to research and write their names on strips of paper. When their names are called, they tape their strips beside their first choices. If the first choice is taken, they go to the second choice, etc. **Webbing:** After playing "Twenty questions," students create a class web by: ● Working in teams to write questions about animals on individual strips of paper. ● Grouping the questions into broad categories. ● Labeling the groups, e.g., description, food, behavior. ● Extending the web by agreeing on what needs to be addressed in each category.	**I CAN statements:** ● Share ideas with others in my group. ● Give reasons for what I think and say. ● Listen to what others say and show respect for their ideas. ● Work with my group to complete a task or solve a problem. **Informal checking:** Throughout the process, T and LMS ask questions to see if students understand what they are doing, how they are doing it, and why it is important. **Examination of student work:** Use the web as evidence of students' ability to generate questions and to organize them in a meaningful way.

5. Plan the search and culminating project

Teaching and learning strategies: explaining the culminating project, identifying possible resources, selecting keywords for searching.

T/LMS	Students	Assessment
Explaining product (T): Explain the performance task: to create a book about one of the animals in the habitat. The book will become part of a class library about that habitat. **Identifying resources (LMS):** Have students brainstorm possible resources. Point out the various information centers—catalog, magazines, computers for Internet and CD ROM programs, etc. Explain what can be found at each center. Prepare fourth graders for their roles as research buddies. *(See Figure 7.2. Ten tips for tutors)* **Selecting keywords (LMS):** Model how to generate keywords. Consider the following: • Name of the habitat. • Name of the animal. • Alternative names for the animal. • Name of the species. • Subset of the animal group.	**Explaining product:** Students listen attentively to the explanation of the assignment and respond by asking questions to clarify. **Identifying resources:** They form teams composed of first and fourth graders and brainstorm the kinds of resources that might have information about animals and their habitats. They share team lists and develop a class list. **Selecting keywords:** First graders work with their buddies to develop a list of three to five keywords they might use to search for information. They use a dictionary or encyclopedia of animals to find these terms.	**Journal prompts:** For product— • What will my book be about? • Who will read it? • What would I like the readers to say about it? For process— • What did I work on today? • What resources did I use? • What search words did I use? • Did the information meet my need? Why or why not?

6. Locate, retrieve, and evaluate information

Teaching and learning strategies: note taking using keywords, modeling, guided practice with feedback.

T/LMS	Students	Assessment
Note taking (LMS): Create a form for taking notes and citing sources. The form includes a column for keywords or phrases and a column for writing sentences from the keywords. Give students a separate note taking form for each question on the web. They take notes on one subtopic and use a different resource each day. *(See Figure 7.3. Note taking form)* Explain criteria for good notes: • Write in your own words. • Answer the questions. • Use keywords and phrases. • Include details. **Modeling (T/LMS):** Model the process of taking short notes about an animal from the habitat. Model the process of writing sentences from the short notes.	**Note taking:** In the library media center students read for information and take short notes using keywords or phrases. In the classroom students write sentences from their short notes. The fourth grade buddies serve as guides as students access the different centers. Their responsibilities include: • Explaining the resources available in the center. • Helping first graders to evaluate the appropriateness of the resources. • Coaching students through the process of locating and retrieving information. • Helping students to read for information and to highlight selected text. • Assisting with note taking.	**Guided practice/ feedback:** T and LMS observe, coach, and provide feedback as buddies work with students. **I CAN statements:** • Read to find the keywords that answer my questions. • Take notes that give important information about my topic. • Take notes from at least two different kinds of resources. • Use my notes to write sentences about my topic. **Examination of student work:** T and the LMS also use I CAN statements to assess notes and plan interventions. **Journal prompts:** • What question did I work on today? • What resources did I use? Did I find the information I needed? • What will I do tomorrow?

7. Organize, synthesize, analyze, interpret information

Teaching and learning strategies: establishing assessment criteria; drafting, assessing, and revising; forming generalizations.

T/LMS	Students	Assessment
Establishing criteria (T/LMS): Use models to engage students in a discussion of the qualities of good writing including ideas or content, organization, choice of words, voice, and conventions.	**Establishing criteria:** Students work with a partner to decide which writing samples are "good," "better," and "best."	**Informal checking:** Are students: ● Actively participating? ● Giving reasons for their decisions?
Drafting, assessing, revising (T): Share models of good notes and engage students in a discussion of "good, better, best" examples. Model how to write a topic sentence and supporting details that identify the animal. *(See Figure 7.4. My writing map)*	**Guided practice/feedback:** With their buddies, they assess the facts and ideas included in first drafts. They consider: ● Do I have enough facts and information? ● Did I include enough details? ● Is all my information correct? They re-examine resources to make changes, find additional information, check citations, etc.	**I CAN statements:** ● Write a book about my topic that has interesting facts and information. ● Use information from three resources. ● Organize my writing so that sentences about one thing are together. ● Share what I have written with my buddy. ● Improve my writing by adding more details. ● Correct my spelling, punctuation, choice of words, etc. ● Write in complete sentences. ● Draw pictures to explain what I have written.
Art work (T/LMS): Present models of good illustrations using published books and student work. Help students to determine criteria for visuals in their books.	**Drafting/revising:** They write topic sentences, use notes to add details, and revise drafts incorporating feedback. **Artwork:** They create visuals to accompany each page.	*(See Figure 7.5 Checklist for writing an informational book)*
Synthesizing information (T): As information is gathered, relate it to the essential question.	**Synthesizing information:** They work in groups to analyze the data and form generalizations in terms of the essential question.	**Conferencing:** ● T conferences with students on their drafts. ● LMS helps with resources.

8. Develop and present findings

Teaching and learning strategies: planning to present, writing letters of invitation, assessing the fair.

T/LMS	Students	Assessment
Planning to present (T/LMS): Work with students to plan the Habitat Fair. Steps include: ● Have students select committees to work on—publicity, decorations, library, hospitality, etc. ● Go over roles and responsibilities for each group. ● Help students re-create the habitat in the classroom. Encourage each child to contribute something to the environment. **Writing letters of invitation (T):** Prepare a letter writing form for inviting guests. Design forms for guests to write their comments.	**Planning to present:** Students sign up to work on one of the committees. They work cooperatively with others on the committee to meet goals. They contribute artifacts, crafts, or other objects to the habitat. They complete a book about one of the animals that lives in the habitat and place it in the habitat library. Students write a letter inviting parents to the habitat fair and explain what they will want parents to notice about their respective books.	**Journal prompts:** ● What are the goals of my committee? ● What are my responsibilities on the committee? ● What have I contributed to the habitat? ● How do I feel about this activity? What was fun? What was difficult? **Parent assessment:** A form will be provided in each child's book inviting parents to comment on their child's efforts. Parents will also be asked for their comments on the unit as a whole.

Web for Animal Adaptation

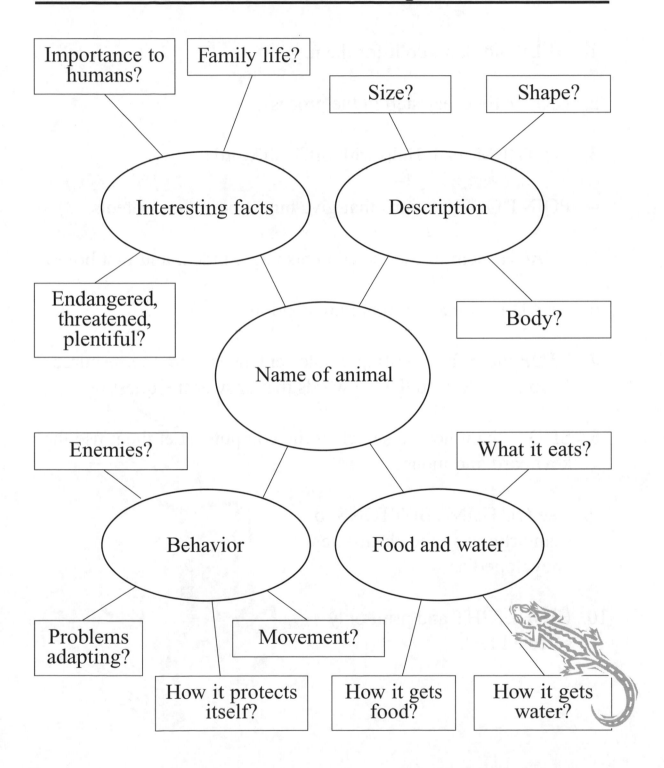

Ten Tips for Tutors

1. HELP but don't do it for them.

2. EXPLAIN every step in the process.

3. Let THEM read. Help with difficult words.

4. POINT OUT captions that give hints about the contents.

5. TEACH them to use the contents page, index, and fact boxes.

6. READ information in picture captions.

7. STOP them from writing whole sentences from the resource. Help them to find the keywords that answer the question.

8. SHOW them how to search at the computer. Let them use the keyboard and mouse.

9. Use OUTLINE BUTTONS to scan articles in the electronic encyclopedias.

10. HIGHLIGHT and print only selected text.

Note Taking Form

Name _____

Topic _____

My notes about: (Circle one)   Description   Food   Behavior

Keywords Notes	My Sentences (I can use the key words to write sentences.)

This is where I found my information: (Circle those used for notes on this page.)

Books   Magazines   Print encyclopedias

Electronic encyclopedias   Internet

Author: _____   Title: _____

Date: _____   Page: _____

My Writing Map

Topic: _____

Use a writing map to plan your writing. It helps you
to organize your ideas and to think of things to write about.

N

W   E

S

What I will write about (description, food, behavior, or interesting facts)	My topic sentence for this section
Detail	Information from my notes
Detail	Information from my notes
Detail	Information from my notes

Checklist for Writing an Informational Book

Criteria	Met	Not Yet	Comments
I can write a book about my topic that has interesting facts and information.			
I can find information in three or more resources.			
I can organize my writing so that sentences about one thing are together.			
I can rewrite what I have written to make it clear to my readers.			
I can share what I have written with someone who can help me to improve it.			
I can improve my writing by adding more details.			
I can correct my spelling, punctuation, and choice of words.			
I can write in complete sentences.			
I can make a title page.			
I can make a table of contents.			
I can tell where I found my information.			
I can add drawings that help explain my ideas.			

8 Profile of a Middle School Project

This chapter highlights a seventh grade project in health education and the dangers of substance abuse. We have organized the profile in a template format under the following components:

- Summary of project.
- Learner goals.
- Culminating product or performance.
- Essential questions.
- Standards addressed.
- Assessment criteria and methods.
- Resources.
- Teaching strategies and procedures.

For more information on the organization of this chapter, refer to the introduction to chapter 7.

Grade 7—Avoiding harmful substances

Summary of project

Theme or issue: Becoming a healthier you—avoiding harmful substances.

Grade level or course: Grade 7, interdisciplinary.

Duration of project: One semester.

Students are invited to participate in a "Healthy Kids" wellness fair to be staged at the local town center. To investigate healthier lifestyles, they work with their middle school core teachers on a range of issues including a nutritious diet, physical fitness, good hygiene, disease prevention, and avoidance of harmful substances. Each core group selects one of these aspects to investigate in depth. The following unit plan has been developed by core teachers whose students have selected the avoidance of harmful substances.

Learner goals

Content Goals
Students will demonstrate knowledge of abused substances by:
- Identifying substances that are harmful.
- Explaining how and why these substances are harmful.
- Identifying the internal and external factors that may lead to substance abuse.
- Proposing a plan of action for avoiding addiction to harmful substances.

Process Goals
Students will demonstrate an ability to use the information search process by collecting, analyzing, synthesizing, and presenting information related to the theme of harmful substances.

Culminating product or performance

Students develop a visual presentation for a wellness fair to be held at the town center. In their presentation, they must explain why a particular substance is harmful for both individuals and communities. The presentation might be in the form of a display board, a video, a multimedia show, etc. The questions to be addressed are:
- Why is this substance harmful?
- What internal and external influences contribute to the abusive use of this substance?
- What can we do to prevent abusive use of this substance?

Essential questions

Driving question for the semester: What does it mean to be healthy?

Essential questions for the unit:
- What substances are harmful to individuals and communities?
- Why are these substances harmful? How do they affect individuals and communities?
- What internal and external factors contribute to abuse of these substances?
- How can individuals and communities prevent substance abuse?

Standards addressed

Health Standards

Standard 1: Students will comprehend concepts related to health promotion and disease prevention.

Standard 2: Students will demonstrate the ability to access valid health information and health-promoting products and services.

Standard 3: Students will demonstrate the ability to practice health-enhancing behaviors and reduce health risks.

Standard 4: Students will analyze the influence of culture, media, technology, and other factors on health.

Standard 7: Students will demonstrate the ability to advocate for personal, family, and community health.

Source: Joint Committee for National School Education Standards. (1995). *National standards for health education*. Retrieved March 21, 2003, from <http://www.aahperd.org/aahe/pdf_files/standards.pdf>

Standards addressed (continued)

Language Arts Standards

Standard 1: Students read a wide range of print and nonprint texts to acquire new information, to respond to the needs and demands of society, and for personal fulfillment.

Standard 7: Students conduct research on issues and interests by generating ideas and questions, and by posing problems. They gather, evaluate, and synthesize data from a variety of sources to communicate their discoveries in ways that suit their purpose and audience.

Standard 8: Students use a variety of technological and information resources to gather and synthesize information and to create and communicate knowledge.

Standard 12: Students use spoken, written, and visual language to accomplish their own purposes.

Source: National Council of Teachers of English and International Reading Association. (1998–2001). *Standards for English language arts*. Retrieved March 18, 2003, from <http://www.ncte.org/standards/standards.shtml>

Information Literacy Standards

Standard 1: The student who is information literate accesses information efficiently and effectively.

Standard 2: The student who is information literate evaluates information critically and competently.

Standard 3: The student who is information literate uses information accurately and creatively.

Standard 9: The student who contributes positively to the learning community and to society is information literate and participates effectively in groups to pursue and generate information.

Source: From *Information Power: Building Partnerships for Learning* by American Association of School Librarians and Association for Educational Communications and Technology. Copyright © 1998 American Library Association and Association for Educational Communications and Technology. Reprinted by permission of the American Library Association.

Assessment

Criteria	Methods
Content skills Students will demonstrate understanding of how abused substances relate to the larger issues of good health by: ● Identifying factors that contribute to substance abuse. ● Analyzing the effects of substance abuse on individual and community health. ● Working cooperatively to promote health by providing information related to abused substances. **Process skills** Students will demonstrate skill in: ● Collecting, analyzing, and synthesizing data related to substance abuse. ● Using information from a variety of sources to build knowledge related to substance abuse. ● Using the communication process to explain the problem. ● Using the writing process to present information related to the problem. ● Using visuals to enhance a presentation. ● Presenting information accurately, creatively, and effectively.	**Setting criteria** Students work cooperatively to set criteria for both content and process. Example: *I will learn about:* ● *The substances that are frequently abused.* ● *The reasons for abusing certain substances.* ● *Things that can be done to prevent substance abuse.* *I will learn how to:* ● *Select an abused substance to research.* ● *Ask questions about the topic.* ● *Collect and analyze information from many different sources.* ● *Plan how to share the information.* ● *Use my notes to write about the topic.* ● *Create a visual display that shows the dangers of substance abuse and suggests what can be done about the problem.* ● *Talk about our project with people who visit our display at the wellness fair.* **Tools and strategies** The following strategies are used to monitor learning and plan interventions: ● A planning form that breaks down the tasks involved. ● Journals where students record what they are learning, questions they have, and problems that present themselves. ● Conferences where teacher and library media specialist check on both content and process development. ● Rubrics to assess the process and the product.

Possible Resources

Internet Resources

- *ADOL: Adolescence Directory On-Line* at <http://education.indiana.edu/cas/adol/adol.html>
- *Al-Anon and Alateen* at <http://Al-Anon-Alateen.org/>
- *Children Now* at <http://talkingwithkids.org>
- *Infoplease.com* at <http://www.infoplease.com/ce6/sci/AO857824.html>
- *National Adolescent Health Information Center* at <http://youth.ucsf.edu/nahic/links.html>
- *Tips4Youth* at <http://www.cdc.gov/tobacco/tips4youth.htm>

Additional Resources

- Local and national organizations that deal with abused substances such as Alateen.
- Informational books.
- Periodical databases.
- CD-ROM programs including electronic encyclopedias.

Strategies and procedures

T = teacher
LMS = library media specialist

1. Generate interest, curiosity

Teaching and learning strategies: brainstorming, webbing, journal writing, modeling, guided practice.

T/LMS	Students	Assessment
Brainstorming (T): Engage students in a discussion of recent articles in the local newspaper dealing with issues of drug abuse, drinking and driving, and smoking. Introduce the driving question: *What does it mean to be healthy?* **Webbing (T/LMS):** Review the procedure for webbing: • Brainstorm all ideas. • Group similar ideas. • Label groups. Synthesize discussion by helping students to identify the elements common to all of their webs. Present the culminating activity — a presentation at the wellness fair. Explain that students will need to decide as a class which aspect of wellness to investigate.	**Brainstorming:** Students work in small groups to brainstorm ideas generated by the driving question. **Webbing:** Each group creates a web with the question, "What does it mean to be healthy?" in the center. Each group presents its web to the entire class. *(See Figure 8.1. Web — brainstorming key ideas related to essential question)* Students create a class web that reflects all the key ideas. Each group selects an aspect of a healthy lifestyle to investigate. Note: This unit focuses on the group that selected avoidance of harmful substances.	**Informal checking:** Are students: • Participating in the discussion? • Honoring all points of view? • Making sure the web contains the major elements of a healthy lifestyle? **Journal prompt:** What does being healthy mean to me?

2. Explore the theme or problem

Teaching and learning strategies: read-in activity, journal writing, modeling, guided practice.

T/LMS	Students	Assessment
Read-in (LMS): Select resources dealing with harmful substances and set up stations in the library with these resources. Review the read-in process: select, read, write, share. Model each step. Orchestrate the process.	**Read-in:** Students select something to read. They read for five minutes. They write on an index card something new and interesting that was learned. They share thoughts about the resource with groups. Note: This process is repeated three times. Each time students move to a new station and read different materials.	**Informal checking:** Are students: • Selecting materials appropriate to their reading levels? • Focusing on reading the material or are they just turning pages? • Practicing good communication skills as they share what they have read? **Journal prompts:** • Based on what I read today, how serious is the problem of substance abuse? • Which resources were most interesting and informative? • What questions do I have?

3. Generate questions, predictions

Teaching and learning strategies: brainstorming, journal writing, modeling, guided practice, generating questions that begin with *who, what, where, when, why, how,* and *what if.*

T/LMS	Students	Assessment
Generating questions (T/LMS): Ask students to share questions from their journal entries.	**Generating questions:** In small groups, students share questions from their journal entries.	**Informal checking:** Ask students: • The answer to this question suggests that [specify a drug] is a harmful substance. What is a good follow-up to that question? • I see questions asking "who" and "what" but I don't see any that ask "why" or "how"? How might you build in these other questions?
Review agreements for brainstorming, and ask students to brainstorm a list of questions about harmful substances. Points to keep in mind: • Honor all ideas. (More is better.) • No editing until list is complete.	They expand the list of questions by "piggy-backing" on questions asked by others. *(See Figure 8.2. Using the six W's to generate questions)* Students identify criteria for good questions: • Target basic information. • Include "how" and "why" as well as "who" and "what" questions. • Lead to deeper levels of understanding.	**Examination of student work:** Examine the list of questions submitted by each group. Use agreed-upon criteria to provide feedback. If necessary, use student-generated questions as the basis for a mini-lesson.
Explain the function of different kinds of questions in the inquiry process. Model the process of writing questions using Who? What? Where? When? Why? How? and What if? Help the class to reach consensus on criteria for good questions. Lead discussion to determine driving questions for the unit.	They review list of questions using the criteria to determine which questions will best guide the learning and share a final list with class.	**Journal prompts:** • What questions do I need to ask about abused substances? • Which ones are most important?

4. Identify a focus

Teaching and learning strategies: choosing a research focus, webbing, generating research questions using a K-W-L chart, journal writing, modeling, and guided practice.

T/LMS	Students	Assessment
Choosing a research focus (T/LMS): Review agreements for brainstorming before asking students to generate a list of harmful substances. **Webbing (T/LMS):** Facilitate the creation of a class web that reflects the different categories of abused substances and suggests possible research topics. Organize the class into search groups by having students sign-up to work on subtopics identified on the class web. **Generating research questions (T/LMS):** Refer to the essential questions for the unit. Ask: What do we need to know in order to answer these questions? Review criteria for good questions. **K-W-L chart (T):** Model the process of using a K-W-L organizer.	**Choosing a research focus:** In groups, students: ● Create a list of harmful substances. ● Edit the list. ● Group similar items. ● Label each group. **Webbing:** They create a web showing categories of harmful substances. As a class, they combine ideas to create a class web that organizes the study by categories of harmful substances. **Choosing a focus:** In groups, they: ● Select a research focus from the web. ● Divide the work. **K-W-L chart/generating questions:** Students reflect on what they know. They generate four to six questions about the topic. They evaluate and revise questions with reference to the essential questions.	**Informal checking:** T and LMS check for understanding by asking questions and observing group interaction. **Graphic organizers:** Webs created by each group should indicate that students have an overview of the broader issue or problem that includes the major categories of abused substances. K-W-L chart provides evidence of a student's ability to generate thoughtful questions that will guide the inquiry. **Journal prompts:** ● What did I choose as a research focus? Why did I choose it? ● What questions will guide my search for information?

5. Plan the search and culminating project

Teaching and learning strategies: writing a statement of purpose, developing a search strategy, selecting a presentation format, journal writing, modeling, and guided practice.

T/LMS	Students	Assessment
Writing a statement of purpose (T/LMS): Model writing a statement of purpose that describes what students would like to do in their presentations. (Example: In my presentation, I will explain why "ice" is dangerous.) Facilitate the practice session as students write their own statements of purpose. **Developing a search strategy (LMS):** Guide students to develop a list of keywords and a list of appropriate resources. **Selecting a presentation format (T/LMS):** Explain performance task so that students understand how they will be assessed. Share samples of visual presentations to consider purpose, audience, and resources needed.	**Writing a statement of purpose:** Students practice writing a statement of purpose. They use feedback from T, LMS, and peers to revise and improve the statements. **Developing a search strategy:** Students use their own topics and questions to identify keywords. They work in search groups to generate a list of possible resources and the pros and cons of each. They develop a class list of resources under the guidance of the LMS. **Selecting a presentation format:** Students work in their groups to decide how they would like to share their knowledge. Each group prepares a presentation plan for T and LMS approval. *(See Figure 8.3. Planning the research and presentation)*	**Examination of student work:** Each student's statement of purpose will be reviewed by the T and LMS to ensure that it: ● Meets criteria. ● Provides clear direction for the project. **Journal prompts:** ● What keywords will I use to locate information on my topic? ● What resources will I consult? ● Which do I think will be most helpful? Why? **Conferencing:** T and LMS review each group's presentation plan to be sure that the following factors were considered: ● Purpose of the presentation. ● Audience. ● Physical considerations such as the availability of computers, network hookups, etc.

6. Locate, retrieve, and evaluate information

Teaching and learning strategies: using print and electronic resources, taking notes, journal writing, modeling, and guided practice.

T/LMS	Students	Assessment
Using print and electronic resources (LMS): Devise a system that requires students to visit different information centers in the library during the course of the research. Coach students as they work on locating, retrieving, and analyzing information. Provide mini-lessons on evaluating Web sites for authority, accuracy, currency, relevancy, and appropriateness. Address other common problems as needed: • Using the index, table of contents, bold headings, and fact boxes. • Accessing information in print and electronic encyclopedias. **Taking notes (T/LMS):** • Model note taking. • Involve students in a discussion of what makes good notes. • Create a chart as reference for how to take good notes.	**Using print and electronic resources:** Students review information sources. They consult each of the library's information centers to search for information. They identify resources that meet criteria for accuracy, relevancy, currency, and appropriateness. They select and download information from electronic sources. **Taking notes:** Students work in small groups to discuss criteria for good notes. **Guided practice:** Students take notes that meet criteria and use feedback to improve notes. They record bibliographic information. *(See Figure 8.4. Note taking form)*	**Informal checking:** Are students: • Choosing appropriate information resources? • Using keywords to locate information? • Analyzing resources for accuracy, relevancy, and currency? • Selecting resources that meet their information needs? **Journal prompts:** • What questions did I work on today? • Which resources did I find most helpful? • What problems did I experience? • What help do I need? **Examination of student work:** T and LMS examine students' notes and provide feedback based on criteria that include the following: • Information is accurate. • Information relates to the research question. • Information provides examples, quotes, and other details. • Information is written in words the student understands.

7. Organize, synthesize, analyze,

Teaching and learning strategies: assess
organizing and synthesizing information, **formation**

clarifying presentations,
rt, and journal writing.

T/LMS	Students	
Assessing information (T/LMS): Lead a class discussion focusing on: • What substances are harmful to individuals and communities? • Why are these substances harmful? • How do they affect individuals and communities? • What internal and external factors contribute to abuse of these substances? • How can individuals and communities prevent substance abuse? **Clarifying presentations (T/LMS):** Conference with search groups to: • Clarify presentation plans. • Evaluate and organize notes with reference to the essential questions. • Provide guidance.	**Assessing information:** In teams, students respond to the essential questions. They use information gleaned from notes to support arguments. They evaluate notes in terms of relevancy to the essential questions: • Is there enough information to reach a conclusion? • Will the information help us to make our case? • Is all of the information accurate? • How can we organize the information for an effective presentation? **Synthesizing information:** Students organize notes around research questions. They collect more information if necessary.	**nt** gro⸺ • Cl⸺ plans. • Review⸺ • Check for t⸺ ing of major c⸺ as reflected throu⸺ responses to essentia⸺ questions. **K-W-L chart:** In the "L" column students respond to the questions asked in the "W" column. Compare what was learned with what was known at the outset. **Journal prompts:** • Could I relate my findings to the essential question? • Am I able to state my conclusions clearly? • Did I have enough details to support my conclusions?

rubric to assess product and journal writing.

	Students	Assessment
...brics ...ify the per- ...k. Answer ... and address con- *Note: If students are doing multimedia presentations, involve the technology coordinator.* Work with students to determine criteria for presentations. Use agreed-upon criteria to create a rubric reflecting basic, proficient, and exemplary performance. Use the rubric to guide students as they work on presentations. ***(See Figure 8.5. Assessing the product)*** Assess final presentations using the rubric.	**Creating and using rubrics:** Students work in search groups to refine presentation plans. They revise statement of purpose if necessary. They brainstorm criteria for a quality presentation and use a rubric to guide work on presentations. They create a team action plan stating: • Who will do what by when. • When and how they will draft, edit, and revise their work. They present their information. They assess the final presentation using a rubric. They reflect upon the process. ***(See Figure 8.6. Assessing the research process)***	**Examination of student work:** Check for: • Revised statement of purpose. • Action plan. • Drafts of presentation. **Rubric:** Using the same rubric, each presentation is assessed by: • T and LMS (also technology coordinator if appropriate). • A group of peers. • Each student in the search team. **Journal prompts:** • How do I feel about the entire search process? • What went well? • What would I do differently?

Web—Brainstorming Key Ideas Related to Essential Question

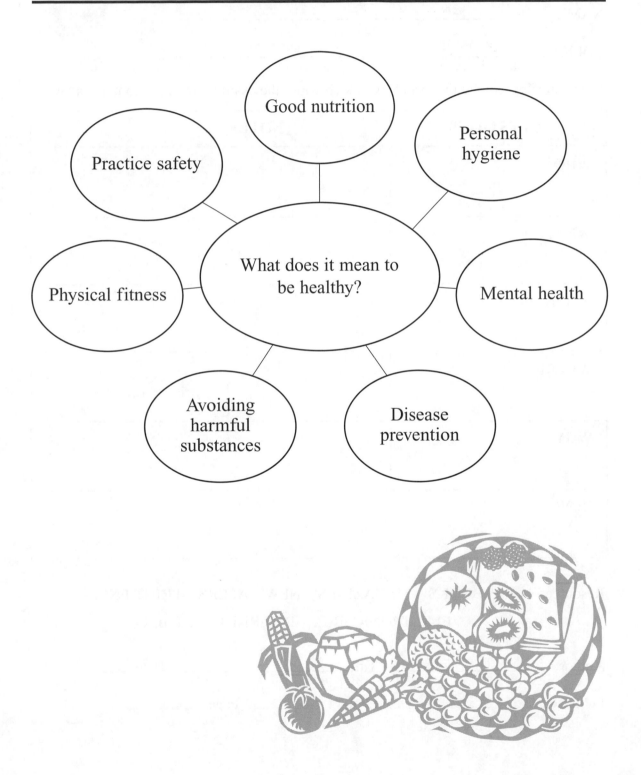

Using the Six Ws to Generate Questions

NAME: _____

TOPIC: _____

Note: Students coined the term "six W's" because they said "how" also contains a "w."

QUESTIONS	NOTES
WHO	
WHAT	
WHEN	
WHERE	
WHY	
HOW	

Resources used: BOOKS   MAGAZINES   NEWSPAPERS   PRINT ENC.
ELECTRONIC ENC.   INTERNET   OTHER

Author: _____ Title: _____ Date: _____

Publisher: _____ Vol.: _____ Page: _____

Planning the Research and Presentation

Topic: _____

Search team members: _____

Our Search Strategy

Keywords for searching: _____

Resources to consult: _____

Our Presentation Plan

How we will share our knowledge: _____

Final due date: _____

WHO	Will do WHAT	By WHEN	Teacher's Initials

An action plan will help you to organize your group project. This is how it works:

1. List all the tasks that need to be done to complete the project.
2. Plan backwards from the final due date and write the tasks in the WHAT column.
3. Assign a completion date for each task.
4. Decide who will be responsible for each task.
5. Get the teacher to sign off on each completed task.

Figure 8.4: Note Taking Form

Note Taking Form

NAME: _____ TOPIC: _____

RESEARCH QUESTION: _____

Facts from the resources	Details and examples to support facts

Resources used: BOOKS   MAGAZINES   PRINT ENCYCLOPEDIAS

ELECTRONIC ENCYCLOPEDIAS   INTERNET   OTHER

Author: _____ Title: _____ Date: _____

Publisher: _____Vol.: _____ Page: _____

Assessing the Product— Student-Created Rubric

Criteria	Doing well	Getting there	Need help
Creativity	It is eye-catching. It includes handmade visuals (graphs, pictures, charts, etc.). It includes informative details.	It is neat, but not eye-catching. It includes visuals but some are copied. It has some details.	You walk right by it. It looks like it was copied. It does not show details.
Accuracy	The information comes from a respected source. All sources are given. All conclusions are supported with facts.	The information appears to be accurate. Some sources are missing. Some of the ideas are not supported with facts.	It is impossible to tell whether the information is accurate. No sources are given. A lot of statements are made, but no facts are given to support them.
Organization	It has an introduction that explains why the substance is harmful and tells how big a problem it is. The middle part explains why people abuse the substance. Facts and figures are included here. The conclusion suggests ways to prevent the abusive use of the substance.	The introduction says that the substance is harmful but doesn't give enough detail to explain why it is a problem. The middle part gives some information about why people abuse the substance. The conclusion suggests ways to stop the abuse.	There is no introduction to explain why the substance is harmful. The middle part does not explain why people abuse the substance. The conclusion doesn't say what should be done to stop the abuse.

Assessing the Research Process— Student-Created Rubric

Criteria	Doing well	Getting there	Need help
Choice of topic	Topic is original and challenging.	Topic is somewhat original but not challenging for me.	Topic is something I already know about. Topic is too easy for me.
Questions	Questions get to the heart of topic. Questions branch out and lead to new questions. Questions ask "why" and "how" as well as "who" and "what."	Questions are important to the topic. Questions require longer explanations. Questions ask "who" and "what." They don't ask "how" and "why."	Questions are not important to the topic. Questions can be answered in one or two words. Questions do not challenge me to learn new things.
Notes	Notes are in own words. Notes answer questions. Notes are accurate. Notes include many interesting details and examples.	Notes are in own words. Not all notes answer the questions. Notes are accurate but not complete. Notes include a few details.	Notes are copied directly from sources. Notes do not answer questions correctly. Notes do not contain new facts or interesting details.

9 Profile of a High School Project

This chapter highlights a tenth grade project on global issues. We have organized the profile in a template format under the following components:

- Summary of project.
- Learner goals.
- Culminating product or performance.
- Essential questions.
- Standards addressed.
- Assessment criteria and methods.
- Resources.
- Teaching strategies and procedures.

For more information on the organization of this chapter, refer to the introduction to chapter 7.

Grade 10 —Global issues

Summary of project

Theme or issue: Building a better world—global issues.

Grade level or course: Grade 10, interdisciplinary.

Duration of project: One semester.

In this school situated near a military base, parents of many students have been deployed to Iraq during the Iraqi conflict. Students are concerned about how such world crises arise and how nations attempt to resolve such problems. The social studies teachers devise a scenario where students participate in a simulated United Nations. They identify, debate, and vote on resolutions addressing problems or issues that affect the international community. This unit consists of two inter-connected learning sections:

- Students identify global problems and collect, analyze, and synthesize information related to those problems. They draft resolutions, debate issues, and practice the arts of cooperation and compromise.
- In their ambassadorial roles students also need to become experts on the countries that they represent.

Learner goals

Content Goals
Students will demonstrate an understanding of the problems and issues that affect people around the world by:

- Identifying global problems.
- Explaining the causes of those problems.
- Providing data on how a problem affects people in a specific region or nation.
- Writing policy statements in the form of resolutions.

Process Goals
Students will develop the skills needed to be productive citizens in a democratic society:

- Research skills to locate, manage, and use information to solve problems.
- Writing skills to effectively communicate ideas.
- Oral communication skills to persuade others to support a course of action.
- Problem-solving skills to collaborate with others to find just solutions.
- Interpersonal skills to compromise and cooperate with others.

Culminating product or performance

Students are presented with the following scenario:

As a delegate to the Model United Nations, you will represent one of the member nations. Your job will be to present your country's position on an issue of global importance and to represent your country on issues posed by other nations. Your responsibilities will include:

- Gathering and analyzing information on an issue or problem that directly affects your region.
- Debating the issue with delegates from other countries who may or may not share your position.
- Using a decision-making process to reach consensus on how best to deal with problems.
- Working with a coalition of nations to draft a resolution that serves as a policy statement on the issue.
- Posting resolutions on the global issues Web site.

In your resolution you will be expected to :

- Explain the impact of the problem or issue on different countries or regions.
- Provide data to support your analysis.
- Suggest a plan of action for dealing with the problem.

Essential questions

Driving question: How can we work with other nations to bring about a better world?

Unit questions:
- What are the major problems affecting the international community?
- Why is it important for nations to work together to solve global problems?
- What factors influence a country's foreign policy?
- How are different regions of the world affected by these problems?

Standards addressed

Social Science Standards

Students analyze instances of nation building in different regions of the world. They
- Understand challenges in the regions, including those of geopolitical, cultural, military, and economic significance.
- Describe the recent history of the regions, including political divisions and systems, key leaders, religious issues, natural features, resources, and population patterns.
- Discuss the important trends in the regions today and whether they appear to serve the cause of individual freedom and democracy.

Adapted from Schools of California Online Resources for Education—SCORE. (1996–2000). *Standards for History-Social Science*. Retrieved April 11, 2003, from <http://score.rims.k12.ca.us/index.html>

Language Arts Standards

Standard 4: Students adjust their use of spoken, written, and visual language to communicate effectively with a variety of audiences and for different purposes.

Standard 5: Students employ a wide range of strategies as they write and use different writing process elements appropriately to communicate with different audiences for a variety of purposes.

Standard 7: Students conduct research on issues and interests by generating ideas and questions, and by posing problems. They gather, evaluate, and synthesize data from a variety of sources to communicate their discoveries in ways that suit their purpose and audience.

Standard 8: Students use a variety of technological and information resources to gather and synthesize information and to create and communicate knowledge.

Source: National Council of Teachers of English and International Reading Association. (1998–01). *Standards for English Language Arts*. Retrieved April 11, 2003, from <http://www.ncte.org/standards/standards.shtml>

Standards addressed (continued)

Information Literacy Standards

Standard 3: The student who is information literate uses information accurately and efficiently.

Standard 7: The student who contributes positively to the learning community and to society is information literate and recognizes the importance of information in a democratic society.

Standard 9: The student who contributes positively to the learning community and to society is information literate and participates effectively in groups to pursue and generate information.

Source: From *Information Power: Building Partnerships for Learning* by American Association of School Librarians and Association for Educational Communications and Technology. ©1998 American Library Association and Association for Educational Communications and Technology. Reprinted by permission of the American Library Association.

Assessment

Criteria	Methods
Content skills Students will demonstrate knowledge of: • The issues and problems that affect people throughout the world. • The perspectives of different regions and nations in respect to these problems and issues. **Process skills** Students will demonstrate skill in: • Collecting, analyzing, and synthesizing data for the purpose of solving problems. • Using decision-making processes to resolve differences. • Writing and delivering a persuasive argument based on the interests of a specific nation or region. • Cooperating with other delegates to reach a compromise that is acceptable to all concerned.	**Setting criteria** Students will participate in setting criteria for what should be learned. These criteria are developed at the beginning of the study and used throughout the unit to guide the learning. Here is an example: *As the delegate from _____ , I will learn about:* • *The purpose and the organization of the United Nations.* • *The problems that are faced by people all over the world.* • *The positions taken by different nations or regions in respect to these issues.* *I will learn how to:* • *Collect and analyze the information needed to solve problems.* • *Use information to draft a resolution.* • *Convince the other delegates to vote in favor of the resolution.* • *Work with the other delegates to reach a compromise when necessary.* Additional strategies: • Reflection journals where students "think aloud" about the process. • Informal checking focused on how students are progressing in terms of the criteria. • Examination of student work, including graphic organizers, notes, and drafts.

Possible Resources

Internet Resources

- *The United Nations* at <http://www.un.org>
- *United Nations Association of the United States of America* at <http://www.unausa.org>
- *UNA-USA Global Classrooms* at <http://www.unausa.org/newindex.asp?> Also at <http://www.unausa.org/programs/qcmun.asp>
- *United Nations Cyberschoolbus* at <http://www.un.org/Pubs/CyberSchoolBus/munda/munmore.htm>
- The World Bank Group. *Countries and Regions* at <http://www.worldbank.org/html/schools/explore.htm>
- CIA. *The World Factbook 2003* at <http://www.cia.gov/cia/publications/factbook/>
- United Nations. *Welcome to the United Nations* at <http://www.un.org/english/>

Additional Resources

- Local embassies, consulates, and other organizations representing member nations.
- Informational books and reference materials available in the school library.
- Periodical databases to locate and retrieve magazine and newspaper articles.
- CD-ROM programs, including electronic encyclopedias.

Strategies and procedures

T = teacher
LMS = library media specialist

1. Generate interest, curiosity

Teaching and learning strategies: exploring the media, setting criteria, and summarizing.

T/LMS	Students	Assessment
Exploring (T): Use daily headlines to identify global issues and problems. **Setting criteria (T):** Help students establish criteria for articles on global issues. Select and duplicate two or more news articles. Organize teams to read and discuss the articles. Help students reach consensus on criteria. **Summarizing (LMS):** Review or introduce the "Six W's" as a way to glean pertinent information from a news article. (See Middle School unit.) Provide guided practice as students read a selected article and summarize important information.	**Exploring:** Students follow the news media for events that have global meaning. **Setting criteria:** In small groups, students examine articles and determine criteria for a global issue. They report criteria to the larger group and reach consensus on the criteria. Example: • It deals with an important issue (e.g., human rights, peace). • The issue is current. • It affects people around the world. **Summarizing:** Students select, read, and summarize news articles using the "six W's" as a guide. In groups, they decide which issues should be presented to the class for further discussion and analysis.	**Informal checking:** Are students: • Identifying criteria to study global issues? • Using the criteria to select important issues? **Journal prompts:** • What news article did I select? • What problem does it examine? • Why do I think this is an important issue for the international community? **Examination of student work:** The selection of articles will be assessed using the criteria agreed upon by the class. Completion of a "Six W's" organizer will indicate whether students are able to extract pertinent information from the article.

2. Explore the theme or problem

Teaching and learning strategies: exploring the Internet, and evaluating Web sites.

T/LMS	Students	Assessment
Exploring Internet (T/LMS): Demonstrate Internet searches using both Web addresses and keywords. Help students to identify criteria for evaluating Web sites by comparing two pages on the same topic. Have each team search for information on one of the topics identified by the class.	**Evaluating Web sites:** Students brainstorm the criteria for selecting a Web site. The criteria are posted on a chart for all to use. Example: • It deals with the topic. • The information seems to be accurate. • It is attractive and easy to use. • We can read it. • The person or group that created it is qualified to talk about the topic. They use different search engines to locate articles on their assigned topic. Each student on the team downloads an article to share with the group. They summarize and present findings to the class.	**Informal checking:** Are students: • Locating Web sites by address and by keywords? • Using criteria to select appropriate sites? **Journal prompts:** • What search engine(s) did I use? What search words did I try? Did I find what I was looking for? • How did I decide which articles to download? Note: The articles printed out will indicate whether students are selecting Web sites based upon accuracy, relevance, and appropriateness.

3. Generate questions, predictions

Teaching and learning strategies: modeling and guided practice, interaction, and generating questions.

T/LMS	Students	Assessment
Modeling (T/LMS): Explain that different kinds of questions are needed to fully investigate the issue: Factual — begin with "who, what, where, when." Procedural — ask "how." Interpretive — wonder "why." Predictive — ask "what if." Introduce the *United Nations Cyberschoolbus* Web site at \<http:www.un.org/Pubs/ CyberSchoolBus/munda/ munmore.htm\> Call attention to questions addressing political, economic, social, and economic issues. **Guided practice with feedback (T/LMS):** Facilitate the interaction as students develop a list of questions to guide the research on global issues.	**Generating questions:** In teams, students generate questions that are: ● Factual, procedural, interpretive, and predictive in nature. ● Essential to the problem solving process. Questions may include ● Why is it a problem? ● What is the extent of the problem? ● What are the causes of the problem? ● What are the effects of the problem? ● Who is affected by the problem? ● How can we solve the problem? ● What will happen if the problem is ignored? They re-examine their list of questions after reviewing questions posed on the *United Nations Cyberschoolbus* Web site.	**Examination of student work:** Are different kinds of questions asked (factual, procedural, interpretive, and predictive)? Are students able to make predictions that can be substantiated through research? Do questions include the key components of a problem-solving model? **Conferencing:** As students work on questions, T and LMS ask questions to assess understanding and stimulate thinking.

4. Identify a focus

Teaching and learning strategies: clarifying the task, narrowing the topic, refining research questions.

T/LMS	Students	Assessment
Clarifying task (T): Explain the two components of the research: • A global issue or problem to be addressed by the team. • A country that is affected by the issue. Provide background on the role of resolutions in the procedures of the United Nations. This information is available at <http://www.unausa.org/education/modelun/resolution.asp>	**Narrowing topic:** Each team selects a global problem to research. Students determine which countries are most impacted by the problem and assign a team member to represent each of those countries. Each student represents the interests of one of the member nations. The student asks specific questions targeting the social, political, and economic needs of the nation he or she represents.	**Examination of student work:** Do questions focus on important aspects of the problem? Will the questions lead to an in-depth investigation of the problem? **Journal prompts:** • Which country will I represent at the United Nations? • How is this country affected by the problem? • What will I need to find out about my country in order to represent it?

5. Plan the search and culminating project

Teaching and learning strategies: developing an action plan, planning a search strategy, and using a decision-making model.

T/LMS	Students	Assessment
Developing action plan (T/LMS): Clarify the components of the performance task and discuss steps leading up to the drafting of a resolution. <ul><li>Research the global issue.</li><li>Gather relevant information about an individual country.</li><li>Use a decision-making process to come to agreement.</li><li>Draft a resolution for other delegates to vote on.</li></ul> Facilitate the development of action plans. Review the social studies standards addressed by the unit. Provide direction for integrating these standards into the research. **Conferencing (LMS):** Conference with each group to suggest resources specific to their problem, e.g., government and non-governmental agencies that can be contacted through e-mail or phone.	**Using decision-making model:** The class reaches consensus on the steps in drafting and presenting a resolution. Example: We will: <ul><li>Research the global issue we selected.</li><li>Gather information about the countries we represent.</li><li>Find out what has been done to solve the problem.</li><li>Find a solution acceptable to all sponsoring nations.</li><li>Draft and post resolutions on the class Web site.</li><li>Present resolutions.</li></ul> *(See Figure 9.1. Decision-making process)* **Developing action plan:** Students draw up an action plan that specifies who will do what by when. **Refining research questions:** They create a web of information needed for each country. *(See Figure 9.2 Web for researching a country)*	**Examination of student work:** The action plans and graphic organizers will serve as evidence of strategic planning. **Informal checking:** Ask students: <ul><li>What resources will you consult for information about your country?</li><li>What search words will you use?</li><li>What resources will be consulted for information on the global issue?</li><li>What are some alternative search terms to use?</li><li>What governmental and non-governmental agencies (NGOs) could you contact through the Internet?</li></ul> **Journal prompts:** <ul><li>How will I contribute to the group presentation?</li><li>What questions do I have about the content or the process?</li></ul>

6. Locate, retrieve, and evaluate information

Teaching and learning strategies: note taking, using multiple resources, citing sources, and evaluating Web sites.

T/LMS	Students	Assessment
Using multiple resources (LMS): Suggest print and electronic resources to consult. Also provide forms for taking notes for both the global problem and the country research. *(See Figure 9.3. Notes on global issue and Figure 9.4. Notes about a country)* Review criteria for good notes (relevant, accurate, factual, informative, etc.). **Evaluating Web sites (LMS):** Identify Web sites on the following aspects: • United Nations. • Specific global issues. • Countries, regions involved. Use the theme of war with Iraq to demonstrate how to locate UN resolutions addressing the problem.	**Using multiple resources:** Students consult all of the library collections to locate information relevant to the topic and the research questions. They select and download information from electronic sources. They take notes on relevant information found. **Citing sources:** Students cite sources of information. **Evaluating Web sites:** Students use the following criteria developed earlier in the unit to evaluate Web sites: • It deals with the topic. • It is well designed and easy to use. • I can read it. • The person or group that created it is qualified to talk about the topic.	**Examination of student work:** Printouts provide evidence that students have applied criteria to the selection of Web sites. Students, as well as instructors, will assess notes based on established criteria. **Informal checking:** Ask students: • Why did you select this article? • How does this article support your main idea? • Which Web site provided the most relevant information?

7. Organize, synthesize, analyze, and interpret information

Teaching and learning strategies: outlining, drafting a resolution, revising, and editing.

T/LMS	Students	Assessment
Outlining (T/LMS): Provide an outline for drafting a resolution: • Heading—subject addressed and the sponsoring countries. • Preamble—problem that needs to be solved. • Operative clauses—substance of the topic. Each clause contains a single idea and proposes a specific action. **Modeling (T):** Walk students through the UNA-USA Web site, which will be used as a reference as students draft resolutions. (<http://www.unausa.org/education/modelun/resolution.asp>) Provide a template for students to use for resolutions. *(See Figure 9.5. Template for drafting resolutions)* Facilitate setting assessment criteria. Draft a rubric to guide the writing process and the presentation.	**Outlining:** Students brainstorm criteria for the resolutions. They should address: • Ideas. • Organization. • Word choice. • Presentation. **Drafting resolution:** Students use the template and the resources provided on the UNA-USA Web site to draft a resolution. In the process they: • Analyze notes for information needed. • Draft a preamble using the vocabulary provided at the UNA-USA Web site. • Review solutions to the problem that have already been tried. • Support an existing plan or propose a plan of action to resolve the problem. **Revising and editing:** Students assess resolutions and incorporate feedback from teachers and peers into revisions. They post resolutions on the class Web site for other delegates to review and vote on them.	**Rubric for assessing resolutions:** Criteria developed by students will be used to create a rubric for assessing the presentations. Students, peers, T, and LMS, will use the same rubric. *(See Figure 9.6. Student-created rubric for assessing the presentation)*

8. Develop and present findings

Teaching and learning strategies: designing a Web site and delivering an oral presentation.

T/LMS	Students	Assessment
Designing a Web site (Tech Coordinator): Set up a Web site for students to post their resolutions. **Delivering presentation (T/LMS):** Plan a United Nations Day for students to present and vote on resolutions.	**Posting on Web site:** Each team posts a resolution concerning the global issue they researched. Students read and discuss these resolutions prior to voting on United Nations Day. **Delivering presentation:** Students participate in the Model United Nations by: ● Reading their resolutions. ● Answering questions posed by delegates from other countries. ● Debating issues. ● Voting to accept or reject resolutions.	**Journal prompts:** ● What parts of the project went well? ● What did I learn? ● What problems did I have? ● How can the project be improved?

Decision-Making Process

1. State the global problem.

2. Find out what has been tried in the past.

3. Brainstorm possible solutions.

4. Consider pros and cons for each solution.

SOLUTIONS	PROS	CONS
Solution A		
Solution B		
Solution C		

5. Choose the most workable solution and amend it so that it is acceptable to all delegates involved.

6. Determine steps that need to be taken by the international community to address the problem.

Web for Researching a Country

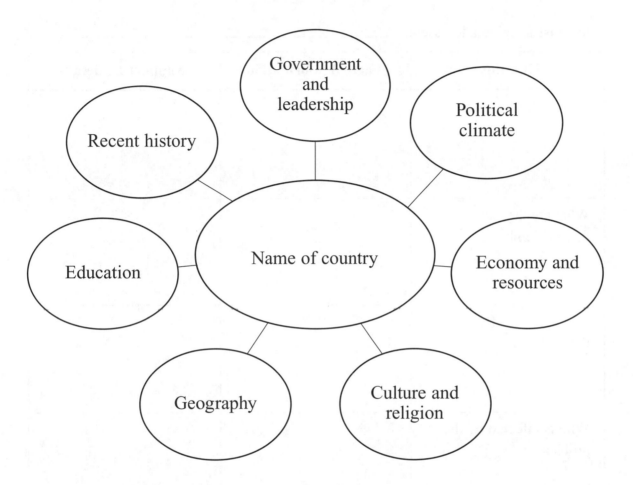

Directions for creating web:
- Review the social studies content standards that are being addressed.
- Determine the kinds of information needed to address the global issue.
- Select labels for each information category.
- Indicate subcategories by branching out as needed.

Notes on the Global Issue

Global issue being addressed: _____

Questions	Factual information	Supporting details
Why is this a problem?		
What are the causes of the problem?		
What are the effects of the problem?		
Who is affected by the problem?		
How can the problem be solved?		
What will happen if the problem is ignored?		

Figure 9.4: Notes About a Country

Notes About a Country

Name of the country: _____

Global issue being addressed: _____

Questions	Factual information	Supporting details
Government and leadership		
Recent history		
Political climate		
Economy and resources		
Culture and religion		
Education		

Note: Students select from the web those categories that represent challenges to the nation they represent.

Template for Drafting Resolutions

HEADING

Subject (The issue or problem):

Sponsors (Nations supporting the resolution):

PREAMBLE

Show that there is a problem that needs to be addressed by the United Nations.
Make general statements about the significance of the problem.
Refer to past resolutions or actions taken by the United Nations or other agencies.

OPERATIVE CLAUSES

Lay out actions needed to achieve your main policy goals on the topic.
Follow a logical sequence in laying out steps to be taken.
Express a single idea in each clause.
Begin each clause with a number and separate with semicolons.

Refer to UNA-USA Model U.N.: Resolution Writing for vocabulary and structure:
<http://www.unausa.org/education/modelun/resolution.asp>

Figure 9.6: Student-Created Rubric for Assessing the Presentation

Student-Created Rubric for Assessing the Presentation

Criteria	Exceeds	Satisfies	Needs work
Ideas	Clearly defines the problem and examines its causes and effects. Suggests a solution. Supports main ideas with facts.	Problem is defined. Some causes and effects of the problem are stated. Suggested solution may not work.	Not clear that the situation is a problem. Causes and effects of the problem are not stated. No solutions given.
Organization (Follows the format for a UN resolution)	Heading states topic and the sponsors. Preamble shows that the problem needs to be addressed. Operative clauses lay out a course of action.	Heading states topic and the sponsors. Preamble asks the UN to address the problem but doesn't say why. No course of action is laid out.	Heading, preamble, and operative clauses are not clearly identified. Reads more like a report than a UN resolution.
Word choice (Includes official vocabulary provided by UNA-USA)	Language is clear and concise. Uses official vocabulary. Wording helps reader to understand the resolution.	Too many words used to make a point. Does not use the official language. Wording confuses the reader.	Does not use the right words to get the message across. Ignores the official vocabulary.
Web design	Page has eye appeal. Bullets or numbers are used to break up long paragraphs. Graphics are appropriate to the theme.	Page is attractive. Bullets, numbers are not used to break up long paragraphs. Unclear how graphics relate to the theme.	Page is not appealing to the eye. No bullets or numbers are used. Graphics are not related to the theme.

10 Moving Toward a School-Wide Approach

I n chapter 1, we introduced the notion of a school that supports inquiry and deeper levels of thinking and learning. In this final chapter, we spiral back to this concept and expand on how such a school-wide effort might be created.

This chapter:
- Identifies action strategies to implement a school-wide approach.
- Presents a scenario of how the strategies might actually be implemented.

What Is Involved?

There are numerous publications describing school reform measures and strategies to bring about school-wide change (e.g., Danielson, 2002; Fullan, 2000; Darling-Hammond, 1997; McDonald, 1996; Newmann & Wehlage, 1995). From these sources, we gleaned the following nine action strategies as essential in effecting changes that extend beyond the single classroom.

Action strategy 1: Create a shared vision (What we believe)
Build a shared vision about the beliefs and values of your school. To make it a dynamic document, the vision must be articulated, explained, supported, and practiced by all members of the school community (Lynn, 1995–96). In some schools, a principal articulates a vision, which is adopted by other members of the school community. In other cases, the vision evolves through a participative process initiated and managed by the principal (Todd, 1999).

Action strategy 2: Define goals (What we want)
Use the vision statement to drill deeper. What skills should students acquire? What knowledge should they demonstrate? What values and attitudes should shape their character and their view of the world?

Action strategy 3: Assess current status (What we know)
Take a hard look at where students and faculty are in terms of the school-wide goals. The process begins with gathering, analyzing, and synthesizing evidence related to student achievement (Marzano, 2003).

Action strategy 4: Select a course of action (What we do)
Examine various curriculum approaches to find the one that best addresses the school's vision, outcomes, and needs.

Action strategy 5: Implement the plan (How we deliver)

Design a school plan to implement the approach or model selected. Successful implementation requires strategic leadership that focuses on long-term outcomes (Danielson, 2002). Leaders may come from the administrative ranks; they may also emerge as the natural outcome of a participative leadership style. Collaboration and articulation are essential in implementing a course of action.

Action strategy 6: Monitor progress (How we are doing)

Conduct periodic review and honest self-assessment. Regardless of the actions adopted, schools need to determine a system of evaluation that measures student achievement in terms of the goals set forth by the school community. The same stakeholder groups, who participated in creating the vision and setting the goals, need to be involved in evaluating the academic program.

Action strategy 7: Provide professional development (How we improve)

Develop a professional development plan, which includes opportunities for the staff to build a knowledge base as well as time for articulation, planning, and problem-solving (Johnson, 1999). Whether the school is building a new curriculum from scratch or restructuring an existing one, professional development is a major undertaking. It is a multi-faceted process that requires the commitment of parents, teachers, administrators, and support staff.

Action strategy 8: Provide adequate resources (How we make it work)

Collaborate on priorities for purchase and access to resources. Since inquiry learning relies heavily on information beyond the classroom, the library media specialist is faced with the challenge of providing diverse resources in multiple formats. Teamwork and communication are critical in deciding how to enable the type of access both teachers and students will need.

Action strategy 9: Acknowledge and celebrate progress (How well we did)

Plan ways to recognize and celebrate school improvement efforts. This is often ignored but it is critical to take the time to recognize how key stakeholders have contributed to successful efforts. This is an opportunity to validate the program and to communicate this good news to the larger community.

What Might It Look Like?

The rest of this chapter presents a scenario of how Oceanview Elementary School implemented these action strategies. Oceanview is actually a composite sketch of several schools where we have consulted and taught.

Action strategy 1: Create a shared vision (What we believe)

At Oceanview Elementary School, the principal posed a deceptively simple question to the group: "What do we believe that children ought to be doing in our school?" The group composed of administrators, teachers, students, parents, library media specialist, technology coordinator, counselor, and secretary brainstormed their responses to the question. Their edited list was summarized in the following set of statements about how students should be learning — students should:

- Use reading and writing skills to build knowledge and explore ideas.
- Be critical thinkers and problem solvers.
- Use a variety of print and electronic resources to acquire information.
- Be encouraged to ask questions as well as give answers.
- Learn to set goals and plan how to achieve them.
- Work cooperatively with others.
- Learn through experimentation, investigation, and research.
- Be involved in the "how" of learning as well as the "what."
- Learn how to assess their own progress.
- Share knowledge with others through quality products and performances.

Using the above statements the group drafted a vision statement and involved the rest of the school in determining the final version displayed below.

Vision Statement

The students at Oceanview Elementary School will be critical thinkers and active users of knowledge. They will learn by asking questions, seeking explanations, and exploring the unknown. They will share their knowledge with others through quality products and performances.

Action strategy 2: Define goals (What we want)

Based on the vision statement, the school determined the skills, knowledge, and values they wanted students to demonstrate. They conducted a series of "think sessions" involving teachers, staff, parents, and students to accomplish this. The outcomes desired are identified below.

Outcomes Desired

We want every student who leaves our school to be:

- *A critical thinker who explores the unknown by asking difficult questions, seeking evidence, analyzing data, and creating his own knowledge.*
- *An effective communicator who uses the tools of written and spoken language to expand thinking, share ideas, and transmit knowledge.*
- *A producer of products and performances who sets criteria for quality work and reflects on his own performance.*
- *A competent user of technology who uses a variety of technological tools to learn, to communicate, and to transmit knowledge.*
- *A truth seeker who creates personal knowledge of the world by asking questions, seeking explanations, and analyzing evidence.*

Action strategy 3: Assess current status (What we know)

The team identified the following strategies to analyze the needs of the school and to assess student performance.

Strategies to Assess Learning

- *Surveys — Parents, teachers, and other staff members fill out questionnaires that are designed to solicit their perceptions about curriculum-related issues.*
- *Observation — Teachers develop observation checklists itemizing specific behaviors related to student achievement. The checklist is used to focus observation on the identified goals, i.e., literacy, critical thinking, communication, quality work, and technology.*
- *Examination of student work — Samples of student work are collected and analyzed to assess the school's current status in terms of the goals.*
- *Focus groups — Focus groups are conducted to follow up on perceptions acquired through observations and surveys.*

Evidence from all of these sources is collected annually. The data are organized and analyzed for the purpose of identifying strengths as well as areas in need of improvement. The process involves the school in a continuous cycle of improvement designed to accommodate the changing needs of students in a growing community.

Action strategy 4: Select a course of action (What we do)

As the professional staff examined the vision, goals, and needs of the school, they concurred that the inquiry approach focused on the questioning, exploration, research, and authentic learning they wanted to establish throughout the curriculum. Figure 10.1 shows how they compared their school-wide goals with the goals of inquiry learning.

Action strategy 5: Implement the plan (How we deliver)

A critical first step in the implementation phase was to have faculty agree upon what inquiry-based units might look like across all grade levels. To accomplish this, they formed committees comprised of representatives from each grade level. In these committees, they discussed, analyzed, and interpreted the standards for each area of the curriculum.

They also met in grade level teams to decide on themes or problems that would help students meet benchmarks for the various content standards. These teams used the work done by the "standards" committees to identify themes and problems that addressed multiple standards.

This work required considerable problem solving and negotiated decision-making on the part of the entire staff. They spent a semester discussing standards and selecting units that would cut across curriculum lines. They also scrutinized their efforts to avoid overlaps and to ensure that crucial standards were not ignored.

Ultimately, the staff captured their school-wide approach to curriculum in a matrix that identified the units at each grade level. Figure 10.2 shows a small slice of the total

Figure 10.1: Comparison of School-Wide Goals and the Goals of Inquiry Learning

School-wide goals Every student will be a . . .	Goals of inquiry learning
Critical thinker	Students identify problems, ask difficult questions, make predictions, design investigations, collect and analyze evidence, and evaluate findings.
Effective communicator	Students use the skills of written and spoken language to acquire knowledge, to explore ideas, and to present findings.
Quality producer	Students recognize and identify criteria for quality products and performances. They use criteria to self-assess and to revise their work. They reflect on their products and performances.
Competent user of technology	Students use technology appropriately as a tool for learning, communication, and presentation.
Truth seeker	Students actively pursue knowledge by asking questions and seeking explanations for real-world problems and issues.

Figure 10.2: Excerpt of Curriculum Matrix for Grades K–2

Schedule	Kindergarten	Grade 1	Grade 2
September	Theme: Life cycle of insects	Theme: Animal adaptation: Habitats	Theme: Interdependence: Life in the sea
	Essential question: How do insects grow and change?	Essential question: How do animals adapt to life in their habitats?	Essential question: How do plants and animals live together in the sea?

matrix—a single unit in each of the grades from K through 2. The standards for the units were too numerous to post on the matrix; however, they were clearly identified in the individual unit plans.

As the library media specialist worked with teachers on the curriculum matrix, she realized that this was an opportunity to align the information search process with the curriculum. Figure 10.3 (on pages 161–162) shows how she took the K–2 units identified in Figure 10.2 and outlined how information literacy skills might be integrated with these areas of inquiry.

Both the library media specialist and technology coordinator also recognized that they had a potential problem on their hands: How could they accommodate the competing needs of different classes and still remain flexible and responsive? They posed the following strategies to the teachers and worked together with them in resolving this problem:

- Develop a yearlong schedule for major units and publish it to the entire staff.
- Work with grade levels or departments rather than individual teachers.
- Address scheduling during planning sessions when all teachers involved are present.
- Monitor the schedule so that everyone has equal access to preferred time slots.
- Develop a buddy system where older students partner with a primary class. This provides one-to-one coaching for the younger child and gives the older buddy another opportunity to show what he knows.
- Be flexible. Most conflicts can be resolved through collaborative problem solving and creative thinking.
- Specific to the library media center: Work the library schedule around the major units. Fit shorter activities like book talks and storytelling into the open slots. If possible, arrange the library media center so that more than one class can be accommodated at a time.

Action strategy 6: Monitor progress (How we are doing)

Teachers and students assessed learning throughout the different instructional units. In addition, the planning teams evaluated the units to ensure that the school-wide goals were being met. They used assessment to:

- Track the achievement of individual students.
- Improve curriculum and instruction.
- Allocate school resources.

Action strategy 7: Provide professional development (How we improve)

The faculty developed possibilities for professional development based on the outcomes targeted for the school (Figure 10.4, page 163). Note that the library media specialist and technology coordinator were key trainers. Assessment was systematically built into all activities. These included rating sheets, reflection logs, development of assessment tools for student use, and school plans for teaching writing.

Action strategy 8: Provide adequate resources (How we make it work)

Collaboration was essential in determining the resources needed to implement an inquiry approach to learning. The library media specialist used some of the following strategies to engage teachers in the process:

- Meet periodically with grade level or department teachers to brainstorm possibilities for themes or projects. Consider the availability of resources before making final decisions.
- Build a library collection by prioritizing purchases that support units identified on the curriculum matrix.
- Encourage teachers to recommend titles for possible purchase.
- Create a selection policy for the school that focuses on providing resources that reflect a diversity of ideas and information.
- Work with the technology coordinator to optimize the use of electronic resources, including the Internet, to provide access to global information.
- Evaluate the collection on a regular basis. Eliminate outdated or inappropriate materials and identify areas for purchase.

Action strategy 9: Acknowledge and celebrate progress (How well we did)

At Oceanview, the staff and students staged an "Inquiry Fair" at the end of the school year. Each class selected its "best projects" to display or to demonstrate for parents and the community. The weeklong exhibit was conducted in the library media center, computer lab, and classrooms. At the end of the fair, the parent-teacher organization sponsored a celebration event in the school cafeteria. Certificates of achievement were given to all the students. In turn, students presented certificates of appreciation to faculty, families, and community members who had helped them with their projects.

Conclusion

Collaboration and team building are the building blocks of a school-wide approach. A successful program requires the involvement of every segment of the school community (Haycock, 1999). The process begins when representatives of various stakeholder groups convene to discuss their common beliefs, values, and hopes in relation to the school. A vision for the school emerges through an interactive process that involves the participants in open discussion, consensus building, and decision-making. Based upon the vision, the school team sets goals, plans strategies, and builds an infrastructure to support the vision.

A well-designed inquiry approach to teaching and learning can help a school meet the demands of the rigorous standards-based requirements that face them today. Thoughtful examination of current mandates such as No Child Left Behind (NCLB) suggests that an inquiry-based approach can indeed advance the goal of improving student achievement. Throughout this book, we have identified strategies that might help schools mesh the demands of school reform mandates with research-supported practices. These include:

- Using inquiry to guide, motivate, and excite students toward achievement of standards.

- Aligning learning activities and assessments with standards and other school goals.
- Providing materials and activities at varying levels of difficulty to allow all students to achieve proficiency.
- Using flexible groupings to address the needs of diverse learners.
- Designing activities that require students to use reading and math skills to learn science, social studies, and the arts.
- Involving students in identifying criteria for quality work at each phase of the inquiry.
- Allowing time for students to reflect on their progress in terms of meeting standards.
- Using technology as a tool for organizing, retrieving, and sharing information.
- Participating in professional development activities related to NCLB and inquiry learning.
- Seeking support of parents by involving them in inquiry learning.

We readily acknowledge that schools may not be ready to sweepingly embrace an inquiry approach to learning. The practical strategy would be to start with a single willing teacher or a core team that is interested in seeking improved ways to achieve deeper learning. They, in turn, become catalysts for instructional change.

When inquiry learning becomes part of the school culture, the library media specialist emerges as a collaborative leader, who engages in "respectful communication practices" that get people working toward group goals (Public Education Network & American Association of School Librarians, 2001, p. 5). As a result, standards for information literacy are integrated with content standards of other disciplines. Ultimately, the division disappears between what happens in the classroom and in the library media center as everyone works to achieve the same targets. As a team, the library media specialist and the teacher provide a learning environment that excites and motivates all stakeholders. What could be more challenging than that?

Figure 10.3: Alignment of Information Literacy Skills with Grades K–2 Curriculum

Information Search Process	K The life cycle of insects	1 Animal Adaptation: Habitats	2 Interdependence: Life in the Sea
Explore the general topic	Take a library tour to find resources about insects. With a buddy read books about insects. Talk about the essential question: How do insects grow and change?	Share books about different habitats. Watch videos about habitats. Focus discussion around the essential question: How do animals adapt to life in their habitats? Use Internet to explore habitats and identify wildlife.	Share books about life in the sea. Watch videos on marine life. Focus discussion around the essential question: How do plants and animals depend on each other? Create a word wall with names of marine organisms.
Find a focus	Choose an insect to study. Write a question that I have about it. Add questions about its life cycle, e.g., How is it born? How does it grow?	Choose a habitat to study as a class. Choose individual animals to research. Create a web to show what we want to find out about each animal.	Select a marine organism to research. List what I know and what I want to find out about my topic. Create a question web to focus search.
Plan the research and presentation	Decide with buddy: • What do I want to know about my insect? • Where shall I find information? • How will I share my knowledge?	Decide with buddy: • What information do I need? • How can I find it? • What search words will I use? • How will I share my knowledge?	Decide by myself: • Search words. • Resources to use. As a class: • Create a matrix to record facts. • Decide how to share information.

Figure 10.3 *continued*

Collect and evaluate information	With a buddy • Identify resources. • Read to find answers. • Take notes. • Tell where information was found.	As a class determine criteria for notes. With a buddy: • Find information in various resources. • Take short notes. • Tell where the information was found.	With a buddy: • Locate the topic in print and electronic resources. • Read and take notes using keywords. • Give title and author of source.
Organize and present information	With a buddy: • Write an answer to my question. • Add details. • Draw a picture to show the insect's life cycle. • Label stages. • Practice reading what I wrote. • Share my knowledge with the class and display it at the curriculum fair.	With a buddy: • Write sentences from notes. • Write a draft for the final presentation. • Edit and revise. By myself: • Add drawings. • Practice reading aloud. • Share my knowledge with other first grade classes and at the curriculum fair.	By myself: • Write sentences from notes. • Organize sentences into paragraphs. • Edit and revise. • Use a simple word processing program. • Use a drawing program (Kid Pix) to create visuals. • Share with my class and at the curriculum fair.
Assess the process and product	Buddy asks questions and records responses to: • What did I ask? • What did I learn? • Where did I find the answer? • How do I feel? (Kindergarten student makes a drawing to show how he feels.) Prepare a process-folio to document progress.	Learning log prompts: • What did I learn? • How did I find the information? • What problems am I having? • How do I feel? Use a checklist to evaluate process and product. Prepare a process-folio to document progress.	Learning log prompts: • What did I do? • What did I learn? • Where did I find the information? • What problems am I having? Use a checklist to evaluate process and product. Prepare a process-folio to document progress.

Figure 10.4: Professional Development Options for Inquiry Learning

Goals *Every student will be a:*	Possible professional development topics	Possible activities
Critical thinker	Thinking skills and habits of mind	Study groups and conferences on problem solving and critical and creative thinking.
Effective communicator	Oral communication and writing skills	Workshops on attentive listening, cooperative learning, oral delivery. Workshops on the writing process and assessment of student work.
Quality producer	Criteria for assessment Tools and strategies to assess	Work sessions to brainstorm criteria for student work in relation to standards. Study groups to examine tools and strategies to assess for learning.
Competent user of technology	Web searching and resources Tools for multimedia authoring Presentation software	Mini-workshops provided by the LMS and technology coordinator on "as needed" basis. Continuing education courses related to technology.
Truth-seeker	Information search process	Workshops by LMS on how to generate questions, plan the search, locate and evaluate information, analyze and organize information.

References

Abilock, D., & Lusignan, M. (1998). Teacher-librarian collaboration in practice: Global warming. *The Book Report, 17*(1), 42–45.

Adams, S., & Greenlief, B. (2001). *Hands across Hawaii: Partnerships for Authentic Learning: Black Mountain projects.* Presented at the Hawaii Association of School Librarians Conference, Honolulu, HI.

Allen, T. (1998). Some basic lesson presentation elements: An outline of direct instruction. *Tom Allen's Net Place.* Retrieved February 17, 2003, from <http://www.humboldt.edu/~tha1/hunter-eei.html>

American Association of School Librarians, & Association for Educational Communications and Technology. (1998). *Information power: Building partnerships for learning.* Chicago: American Library Association.

Andrade, H. G. (2000). Using rubrics to promote thinking and learning. *Educational Leadership, 57*(5), 13–18. Retrieved March 4, 2004, from <http://www.ascd.org/publications/ed_lead/2002/andrade.html>

Brimijoin, K., Marquissee, E., & Tomlinson, C. (2003). Using data to differentiate instruction. *Educational Leadership, 60*(5), 70–73.

Bush, G. (2003). *The school buddy system: The practice of collaboration.* Chicago: American Library Association.

Buzzeo, T. (2002). Disciples of collaboration. *School Library Journal, 48*(9), 34–35.

Callison, D. (1998). Authentic assessment. *School Library Activities Media Activities Monthly, 14*(5), 42–43, 50.

Center for Research on Learning and Technology at Indiana University. (1999–2000). *Inquiry learning forum: Supporting student learning and teacher growth through inquiry.* Retrieved May 9, 2003, from <http://ilf.crlt.indiana.edu/>

Cushman, K. (1989). *Asking the essential questions: Curriculum development.* Retrieved October 5, 2002, from <http://www.essentialschools.org/cs/resources/view/ces_res/137>

Dalbotten, M. S. (1997). Inquiry in the national content standards. In D. Callison, J. H. McGregor, & R. Small (Eds.), *Instructional interventions for information use: Papers of Treasure Mountain VI* (pp. 246–304). San Jose, CA: Hi Willow Research & Publishing.

Danielson, C. (2002). *Enhancing student achievement: A framework for school improvement.* Alexandria, VA: Association for Supervision and Curriculum Development.

Darling-Hammond, L. (1997). *The right to learn: A blueprint for creating schools that work.* San Francisco: Jossey-Bass.

Davies, A. (2000). *Making classroom assessment work.* British Columbia, Canada: Connections Publishing.

Donham, J. (1998). *Assessment of information processes and products.* McHenry, IL: Follett Software Company.

Eisenberg, M.B., & Berkowitz, R.E. (1990). *Information problem solving: The Big*

Six skills approach to library & information skills instruction. Norwood, NJ: Ablex Publishing.

Ennis, R. (2002). Critical thinking dispositions. *WWW links to resources for teaching reasoning and critical thinking.* Retrieved May 13, 2003, from <http://academic.pg.cc.md.us/~wpeirce/MCCCTR/dispos~1.html>

Exline, J. (n.d.). What is inquiry-based learning? *Inquiry-Based Learning.* Retrieved September 29, 2002, from <http://www.thirteen.org/edonline/concept2class/month6/>

Facione, P. A., Sanchez, C. A., Facione, N. C., & Gainen, J. (1995). The disposition toward critical thinking. *Journal of General Education, 44*(1), 1–25.

Friend, M.P., & Cook, L. (2000). *Interactions: Collaboration skills for school professionals (3rd ed.).* White Plains, NY: Longman Publishing Group.

Fullan, M. (2000). The three stories of educational reform. *Phi Delta Kappan, 81*(8), 581–584.

Gregory, K., Cameron, C., & Davies, A. (2000). *Self-assessment and goal setting: For use in the middle and secondary school classrooms.* British Columbia, Canada: Connections Publishing.

Gross, J., & Kientz, S. (1999). Developing information literacy: Collaborating for authentic learning. *Teacher Librarian, 27*(1), 21–25.

Grover, R. (1996). *Collaboration: The "meeting in the middle" experience* (Lessons Learned Series). Chicago: American Association of School Librarians.

Guskey, T.R. (2003). How classroom assessments improve learning. *Educational Leadership, 60*(5), 6–11.

Harada, V.H. (2003). Empowered learning: Fostering thinking across the curriculum. In B. K. Stripling & S. Hughes-Hassell (Eds.), *Curriculum connections through the library: Principles and practices* (pp. 41–66). Englewood, CO: Libraries Unlimited.

Harada, V.H. (2002). Personalizing the information search process: A case study of journal writing with elementary-age students. *School Library Media Research, 5.* Retrieved March 4, 2004, from <http://www.ala.org/ala/aasl/aaslpubsandjournals/slmrb/slmrcontents/volume52002/harada/htm> School_Library_Media_Research/Contents1/Volume_5_(2002)/Harada.htm>

Harada, V., & Yoshina, J. (1997). Improving information search process instruction and assessment through collaborative action research. *School Libraries Worldwide, 3*(2), 41–55.

Harper-Marinick, M. (2001). *Engaging students in problem-based learning.* Retrieved December 15, 2002, from <http://www.mcli.dist.maricopa.edu/forum/spr01/tl1.html>

Hawaii Department of Education. (2002). *Hawaii content and performance standards II.* Retrieved December 1, 2002, from <http://doe.k12.hi.us/standards>

Haycock, K. (1999). Fostering collaboration, leadership and information literacy: Common behaviors of uncommon principals and faculties. *NASSP Bulletin, 83*(605), 82–87.

International Society for Technology in Education. (n.d.). *National educational technology standards.* Retrieved March 4, 2004, from <http://cnets.iste.org/>

Jacobs, H.H. (2000). Focus on curriculum mapping. *Curriculum Technology Quarterly.* Retrieved December 4, 2002, from <http://home.earthlink.net/~carozza/hhj.htm>

Johnson, D. (1999). Implementing an information literacy curriculum: One district's story. *NASSP Bulletin, 83*(605), 53–60.

Kearney, C. (2000). *Curriculum partner: Redefining the role of the library media specialist.* Westport, CT: Greenwood Press.

Kuhlthau, C. (1993). Implementing a process approach to information skills: A study identifying indicators of success in library media programs. *School Library Media Quarterly, 22*(1), 11–18.

Kuhlthau, C. (1994). *Teaching the library research process (2nd ed.).* Metuchen, NJ: Scarecrow Press.

Kuhlthau, C. (1995). The process of learning from information. *School Libraries Worldwide, 1*(1), 1–12.

Kuhlthau, C. (n.d.). *Information search process (ISP): A search for meaning rather than answers.* Retrieved February 17, 2003, from Rutgers, The State University of New Jersey, Department of Library and Information Science Web site: <http://scils.rutgers.edu/~kuhlthau/Information%20Search%20Process_files/slide0013>

Loertscher, D., & Woolls, B. (2002). *Information literacy: A review of the research (2nd ed.).* San Jose, CA: Hi Willow Research and Publishing.

Logan, D.K. (2000). Dear student teacher, you are invited … Educating the future educators. *The Book Report, 19*(1), 15–17.

Lynn, L. (1995–96). Successful school restructuring involves four components. *WCER Highlights.* Retrieved March 4, 2004, from <http://www.wcer.wisc.edu/>

Marriott, C. (2002). Leveraging standards to enhance the library's goals and resources. *Knowledge Quest, 31*(2), 25–26.

Marzano, R. (2001). *Designing a new taxonomy of educational objectives.* Thousand Oaks, CA: Corwin Press.

Marzano, R. (2003). *What works in schools: Translating research into action.* Alexandria, VA: Association for Supervision and Curriculum Development.

McDonald, J. (1996). *Redesigning schools: Lessons for the 21st century.* San Francisco: Jossey-Bass.

Mililani Mauka Elementary School. (1995). The My Search process. *Mililani complex takes a stand.* Retrieved February 17, 2003, from <http://kalama.doe.hawaii.edu/hern95/pt006/LIB/P1/pl.html>

Mitchell, R., Willis, M., & Chicago Teachers Union Quest Center. (1995). *Learning in overdrive: Designing curriculum, instruction, and assessment from standards.* Golden, CO: North American Press.

Muronaga, K., & Harada, V. (1999). Building teaching partnerships: The art of collaboration. *Teacher Librarian, 27*(1), 9–14.

National Academy of Sciences. (n.d.). *National science education standards, chapter 6: Science content standards: 5–8.* Retrieved January 7, 2003, from <http://www.nap.edu/readingroom/books/nses/html/6d.html>

National Center for History in the Schools. (n.d.). *World history standards for grades 5–12: World history across the eras.* Retrieved December 22, 2002, from <http://www.sscnet.ucla.edu/nchs/standards/worldacrosseras.html>

National Council of Teachers of English, & International Reading Association. (n.d.). *Standards for the English language arts*. Retrieved March 4, 2004, from <http://www.ncte.org/about/over/standards/110846.htm>

National Council of Teachers of Mathematics. (2000). *Principles and standards for school mathematics*. Retrieved December 18, 2002, from <http://www.standards.nctm.org/index.htm>

National Geographic Society. (n.d.). *National geography standards*. Retrieved December 6, 2002, from <http://www.nationalgeographic.com/resources/ngo/education/standardslist.html>

Newmann, F.M., & Wehlage, G.G. (1993). Five standards of authentic instruction. *Educational Leadership, 50*(7), 8–12.

Newmann, F.M., & Wehlage, G.G. (1995). *Successful school restructuring: A report to the public*. Madison, WI: Center on Organization and Restructuring of Schools.

North Central Regional Educational Laboratory. (n.d.). *21st century skills*. Retrieved January 3, 2003, from <http://www.ncrel.org/enguage/skills/21skills.htm>

Pappas, M. (1997). Organizing research. *School Library Media Activities Monthly, 14*(4), 30–32.

Pappas, M. (1998). Designing authentic learning. *School Library Media Activities Monthly, 14*(6), 29–31.

Pappas, M., & Tepe, A. (1997). *Pathways to Knowledge™: Follett's information skills model*. McHenry, IL: Follett Software. Retrieved March 4, 2004, from <http://www.intime.uni.edu/model/information/sear.html>

Pappas, M.L., & Tepe, A.E. (2002). *Pathways to Knowledge™ and inquiry learning*. Englewood, CO: Libraries Unlimited.

Perkins, D.N. (1991). Education for insight. *Educational Leadership, 49*(2), 4–8.

Perkins, D.N. (1992). *Smart schools: Better thinking and learning for every child*. New York: Free Press.

Public Education Network, & American Association of School Librarians. (2001). *The information-powered school*. S. Hughes-Hassell & A. Wheellock (Eds.). Chicago: American Library Association.

Repman, J., & Carlson, R.D. (2002). Building blocks for information literacy. *Education Libraries, 25*(2), 22–25.

Russell, S. (2000). *Teachers and librarians: Collaborative relationships. ERIC Digest* (ERIC Rep. No. EDO-1R-2000-06.). Syracuse, NY: ERIC Clearinghouse on Information and Technology.

Short, K., Schroeder, J., Laird, J., Kauffman, G., Ferguson, M. J., & Crawford, M. K. (1996). *Learning together through inquiry: From Columbus to integrated curriculum*. York, ME: Stenhouse Publishers.

Simmons, R. (1994). The horse before the cart: Assessing for understanding. *Educational Leadership, 51*(5), 22–23.

Small, R. (n.d.). Developing a collaborative culture. *School Library Media Research—The Best of ERIC, 2002*. Retrieved December 17, 2002, from <http://archive.ala.org/aasl/SLMR/eric_main.html>

Stiggins, R.J. (1997). *Student-centered classroom assessment*. Columbus, OH: Prentice-Hall, Inc.

Stripling, B., & Pitts, J. (1988). *Brainstorms and blueprints: Teaching library research as a thinking process*. Englewood, CO: Libraries Unlimited.

Tishman, S., & Andrade, A. (1999). Thinking dispositions: A review of current theories, practices, and issues. *ALPS: Active learning practices for schools*. Retrieved May 13, 2003, from <http://learnweb.harvard.edu/alps/thinking/docs/Dispositions.htm>

Todd, R. (1999). Transformational leadership and transformational learning: Information literacy and the World Wide Web. *NASSP Bulletin, 83*(605), 4–12.

Tomlinson, C.A. (1995). *Differentiating instruction for advanced learners in the mixed-ability middle school classroom. ERIC Digest* (ERIC EC E536). Retrieved February 17, 2003, from <http://ericec.org/digests/e536.html>

Unger, C. (1994). What teaching for understanding looks like. *Educational Leadership, 51*(5), 8–10.

Unger, C. (2002). Teaching for understanding—questions to ask yourself and your students. *Transforming Education*. Retrieved March 4, 2004, from <http://www.newhorizons.org/strategies/understanding/unger.htm>

U. S. Department of Education. (2002). *No child left behind*. Retrieved September 19, 2003, from <http://www.ed.gov/nclb/landing.jhtml>

Wehlage, G. (1999). Instruction. In D. L. Zweizig & D. M. Hopkins (Eds.), *Library Power: Enriching teaching and learning* (pp. 101–131). Englewood, CO: Libraries Unlimited.

Wiggins, G., & McTighe, J. (1998). *Understanding by design*. Alexandria, VA: Association for Supervision and Curriculum Development.

Wiske, M.S. (1994). How teaching for understanding changes the rules in the classroom. *Educational Leadership, 51*(5), 19–21.

Wolcott, L. (1994). Understanding how teachers plan: Strategies for successful instructional partnerships. *School Library Media Quarterly, 22*(3), 161–165.

Wolcott, L. (1996). Planning with teachers: Practical approaches to collaboration. *Emergency Librarian, 3*(3), 9–14.

Index